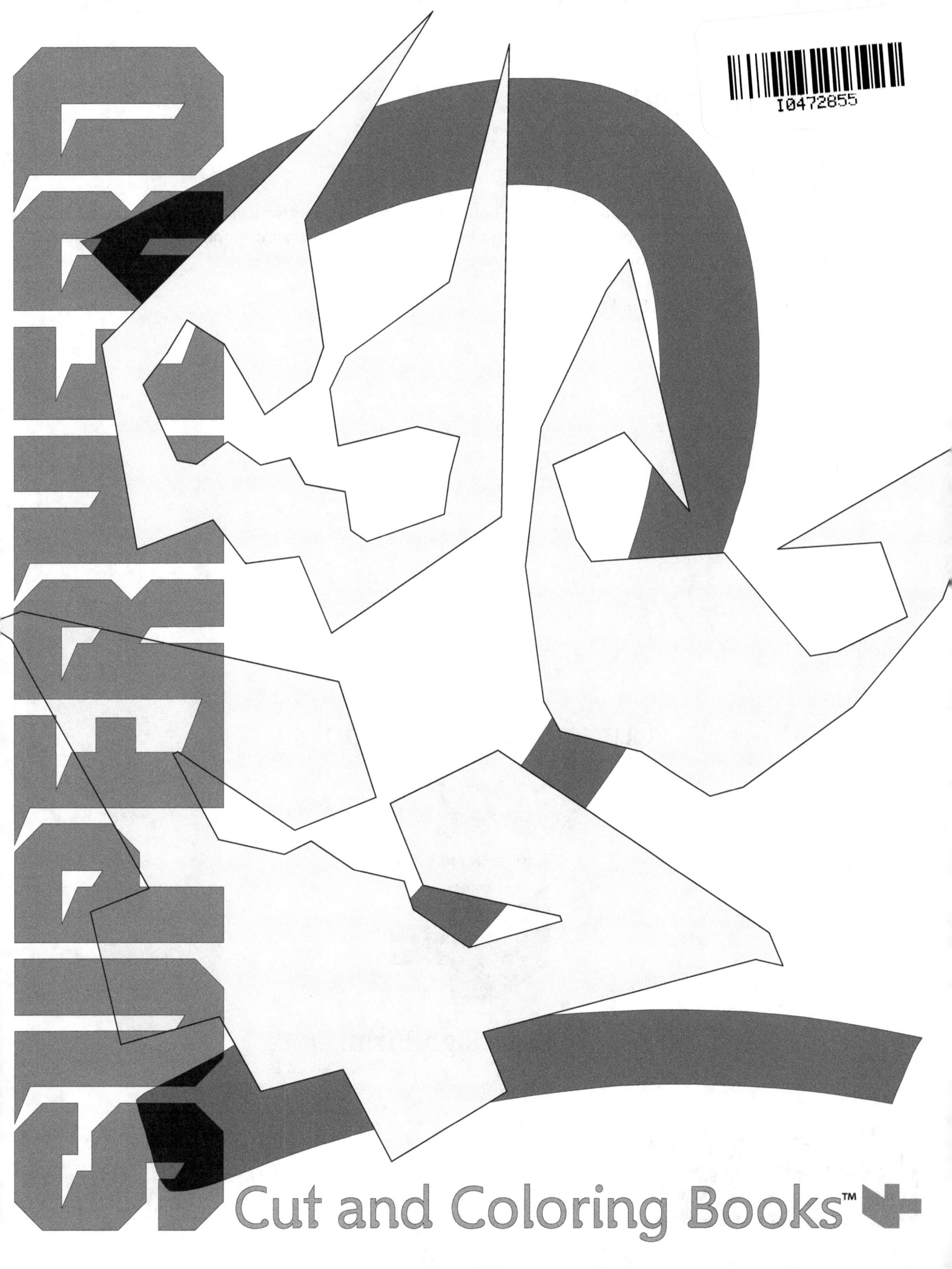

SUPERHEROES

Cut and Coloring Books™

Cut and Coloring Books.

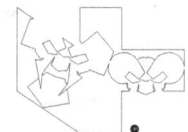

is a complete partner with

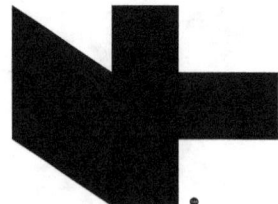

NH Design Firm.

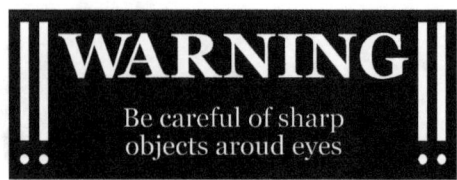

WARNING
Be careful of sharp
objects aroud eyes

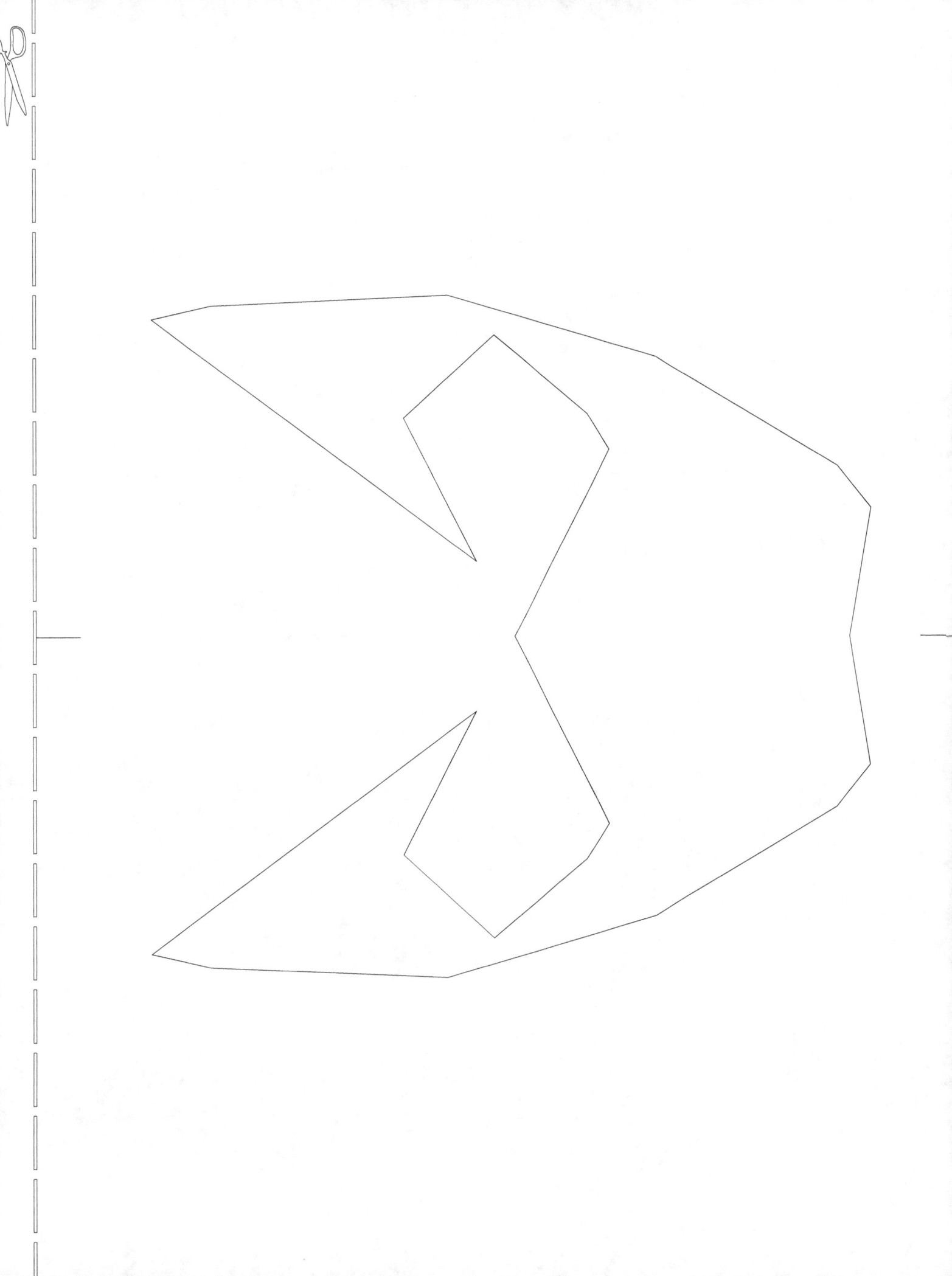

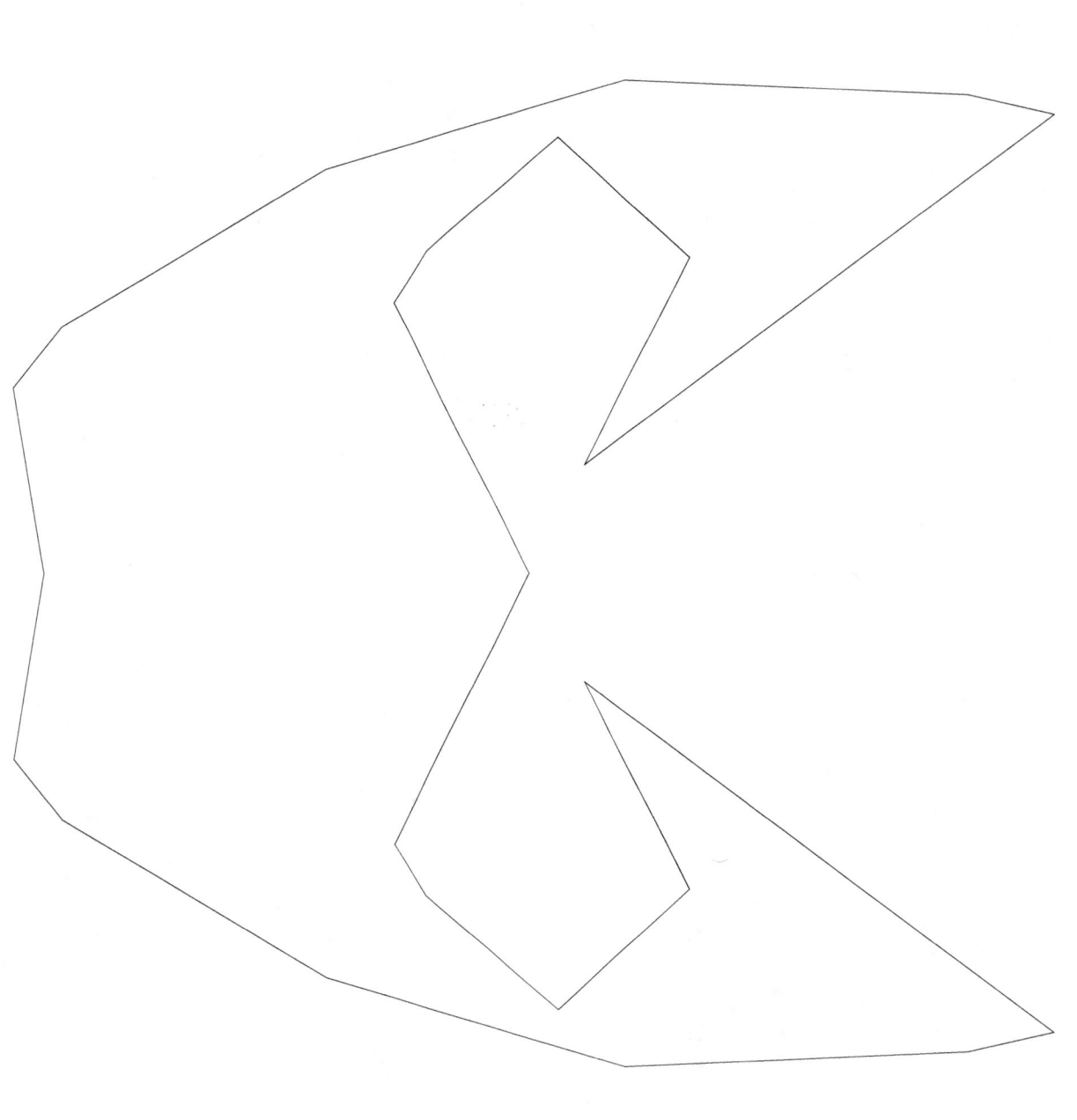

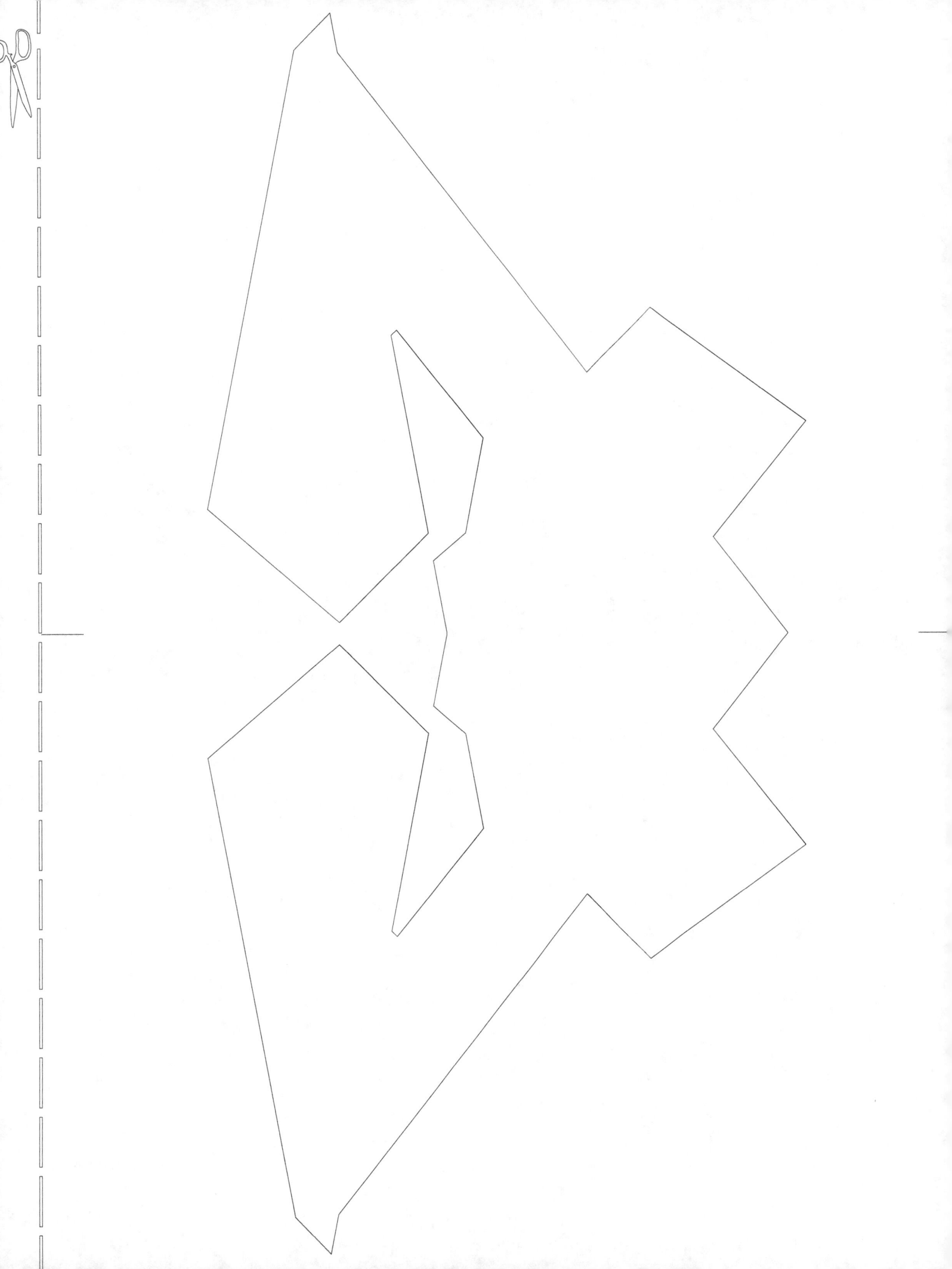

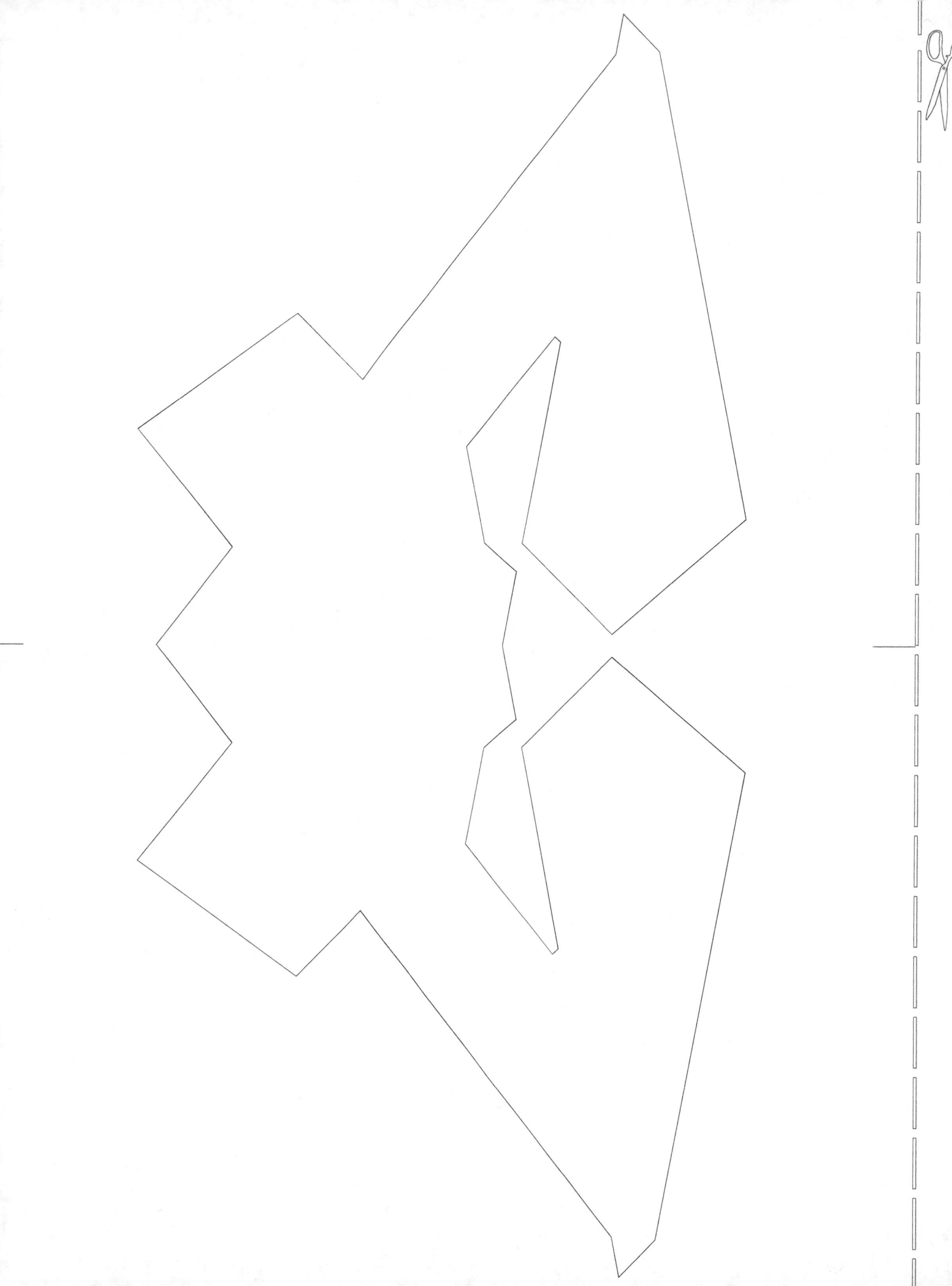

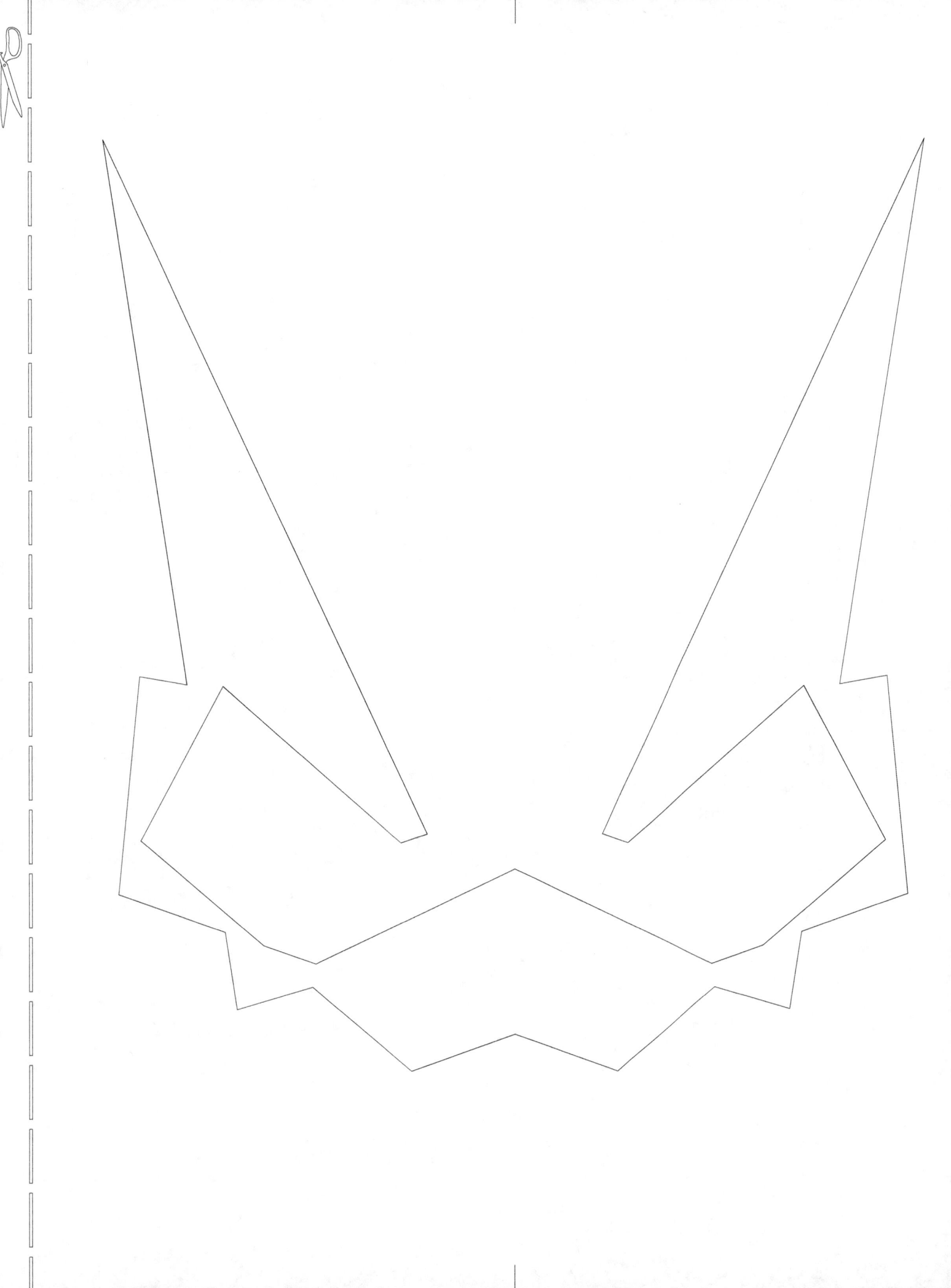

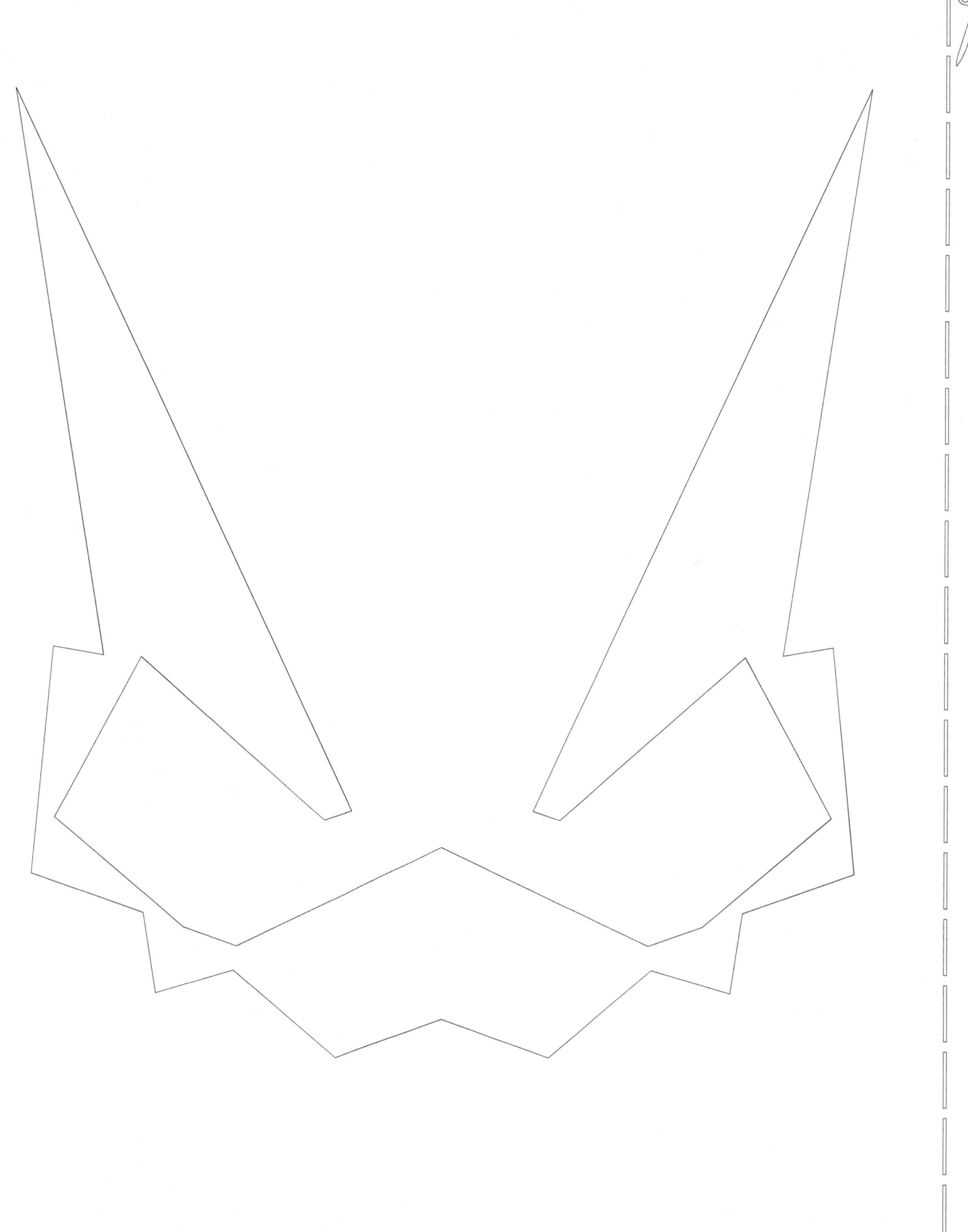

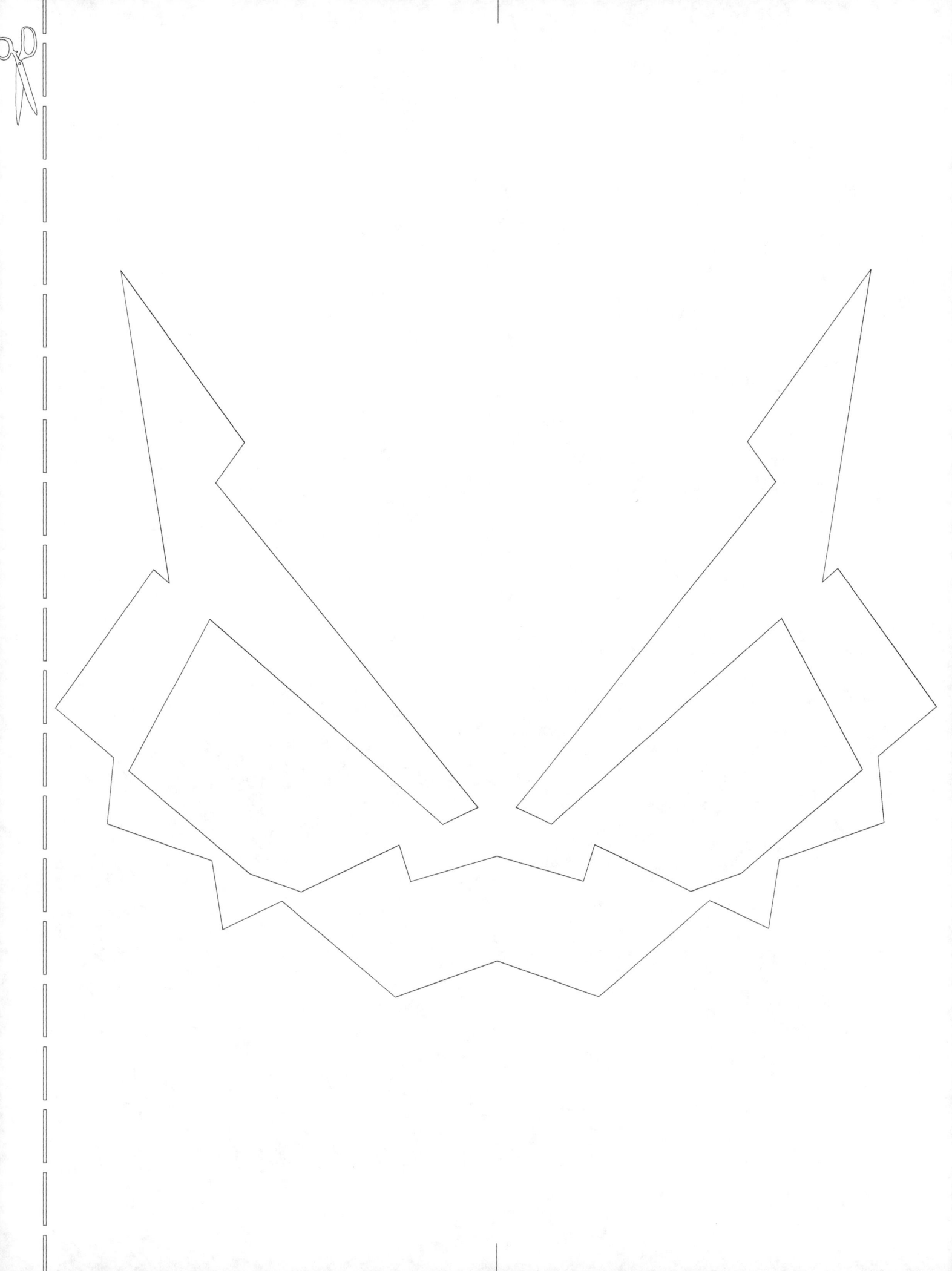

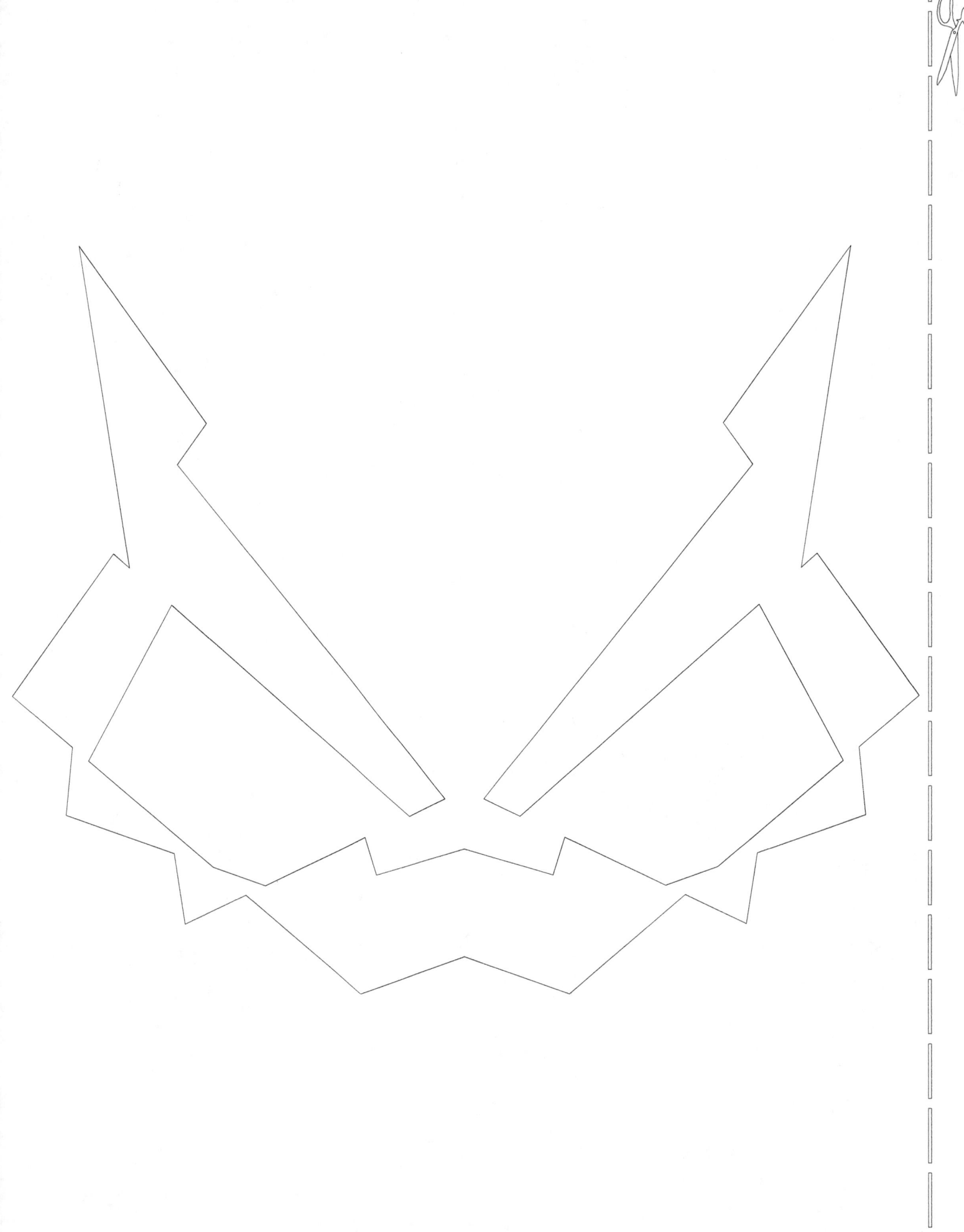

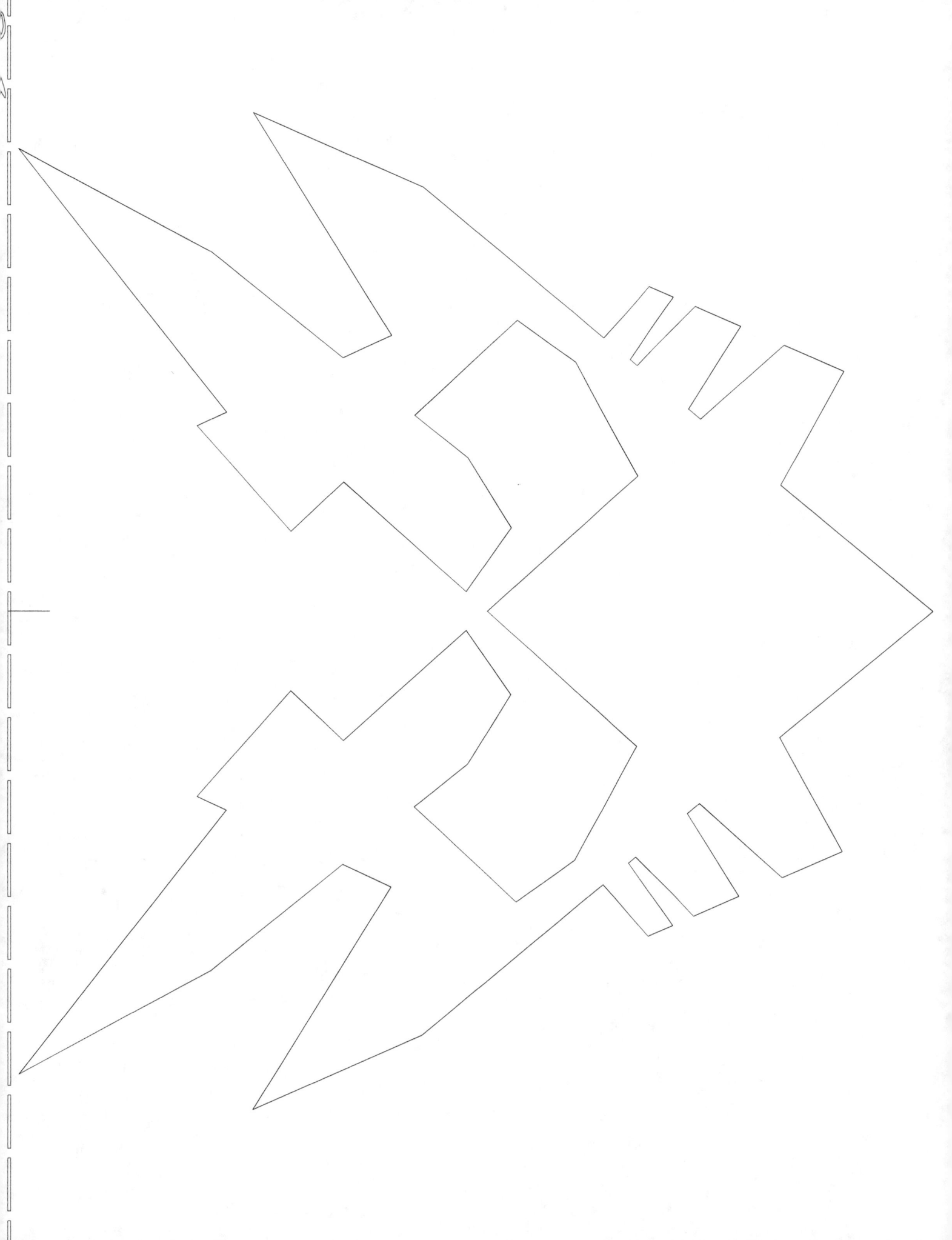

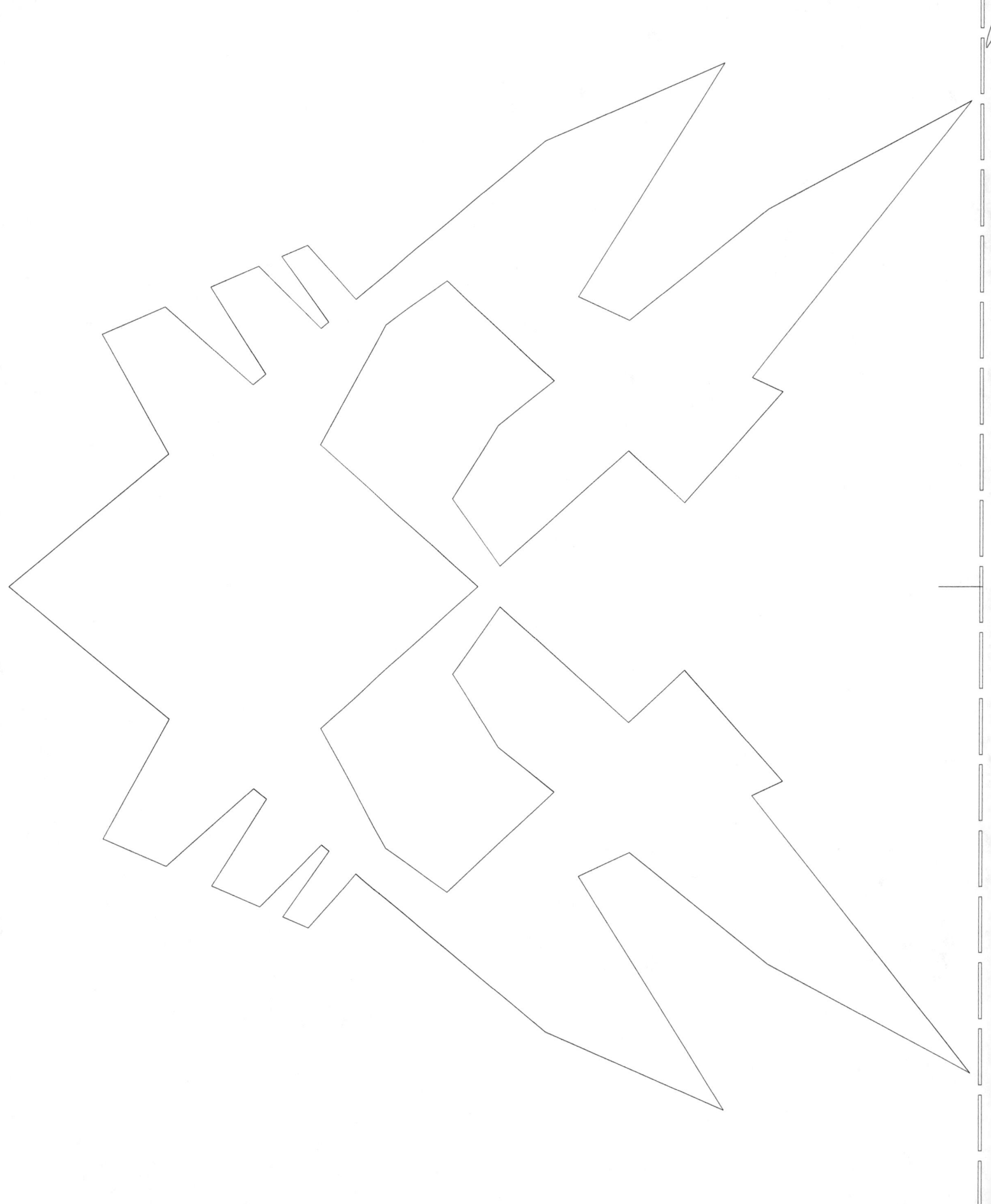

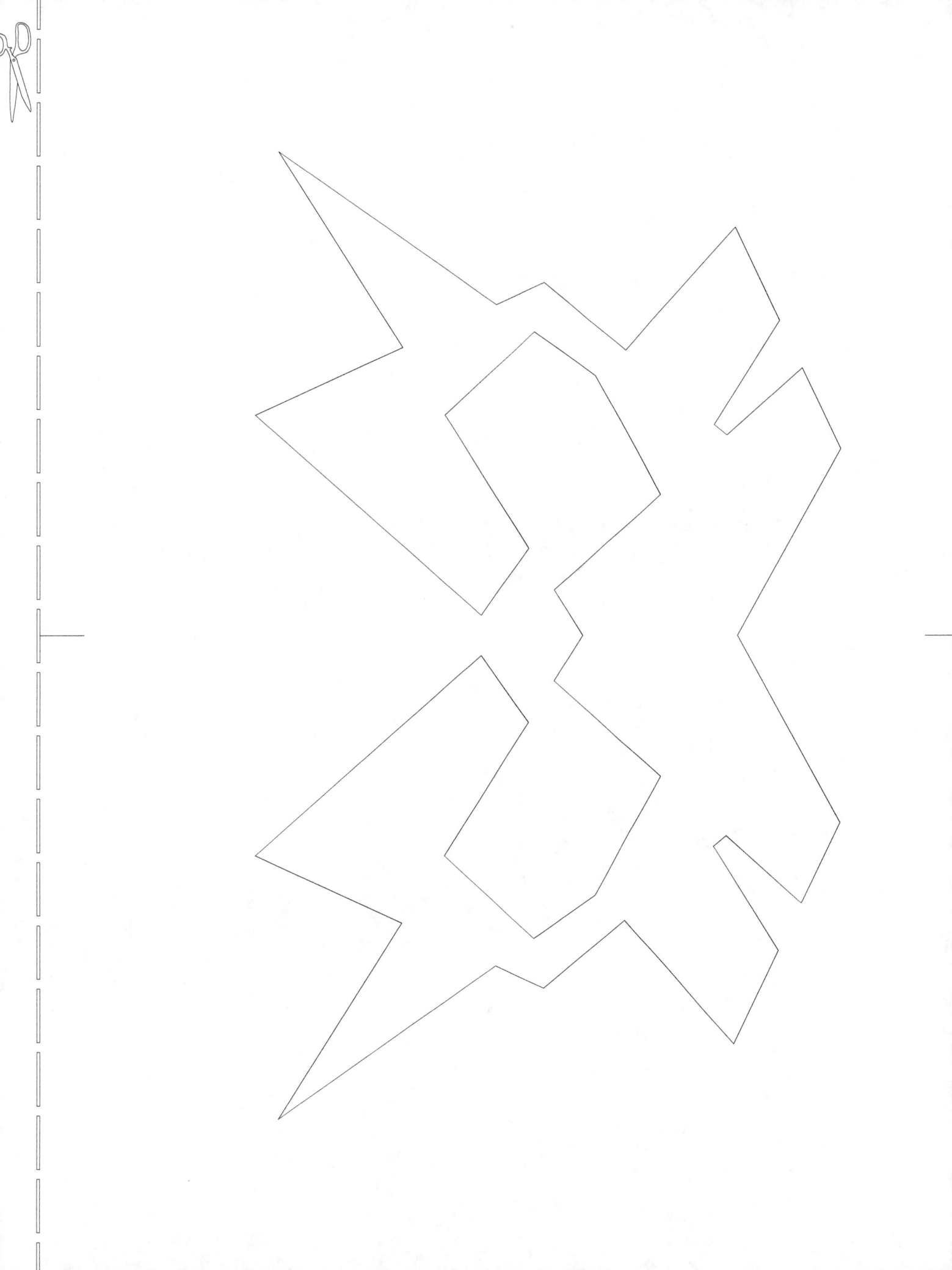

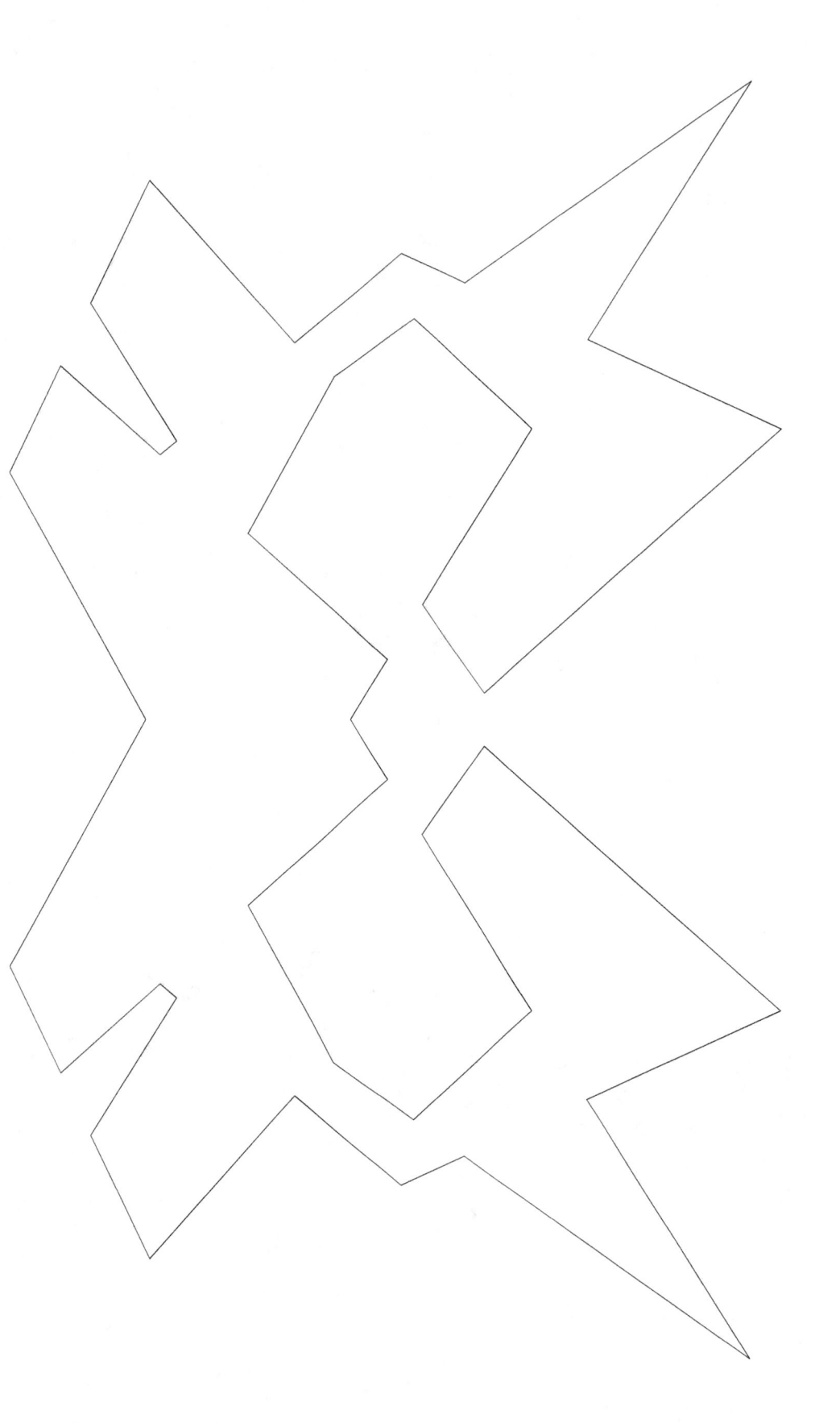

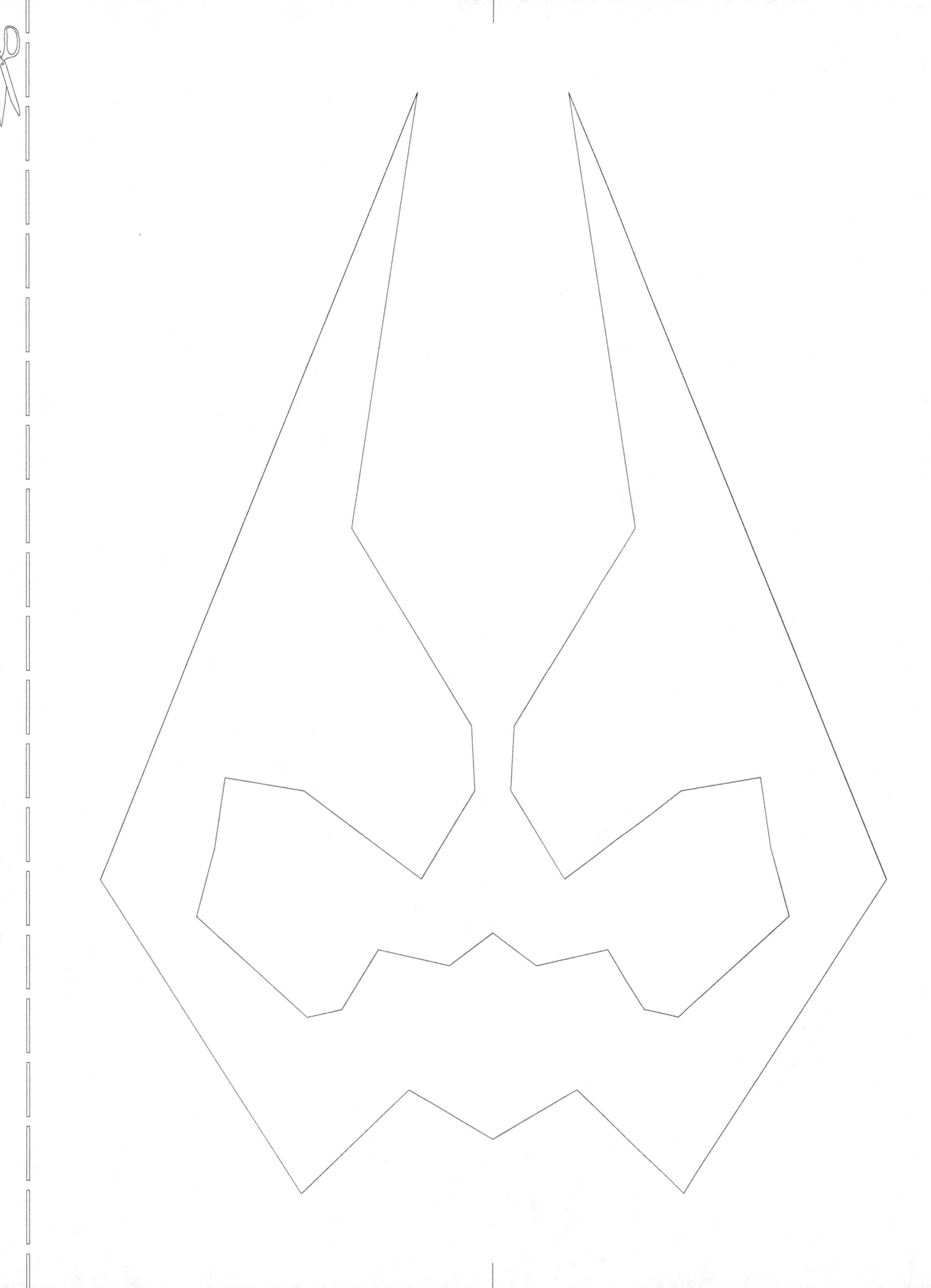

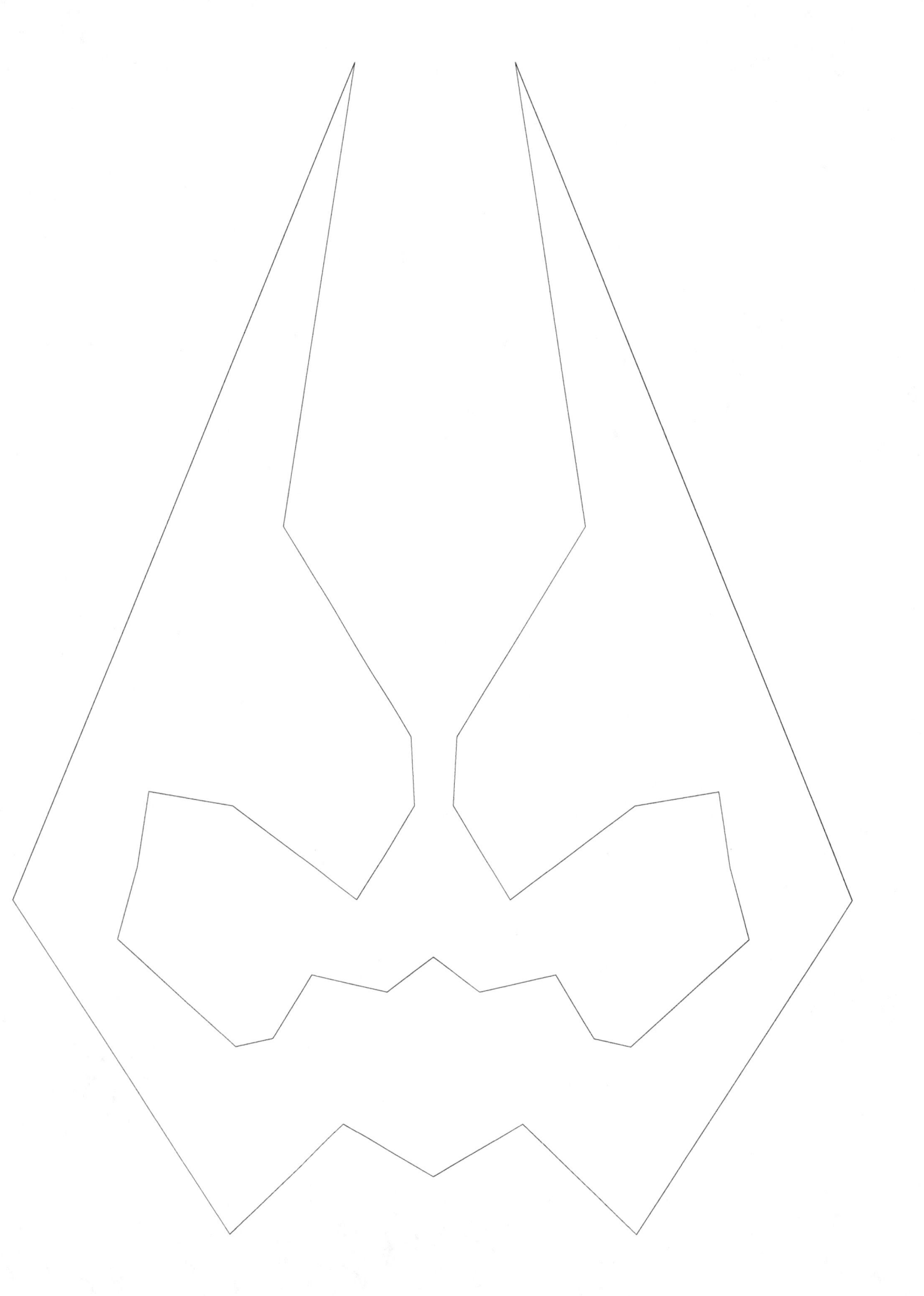

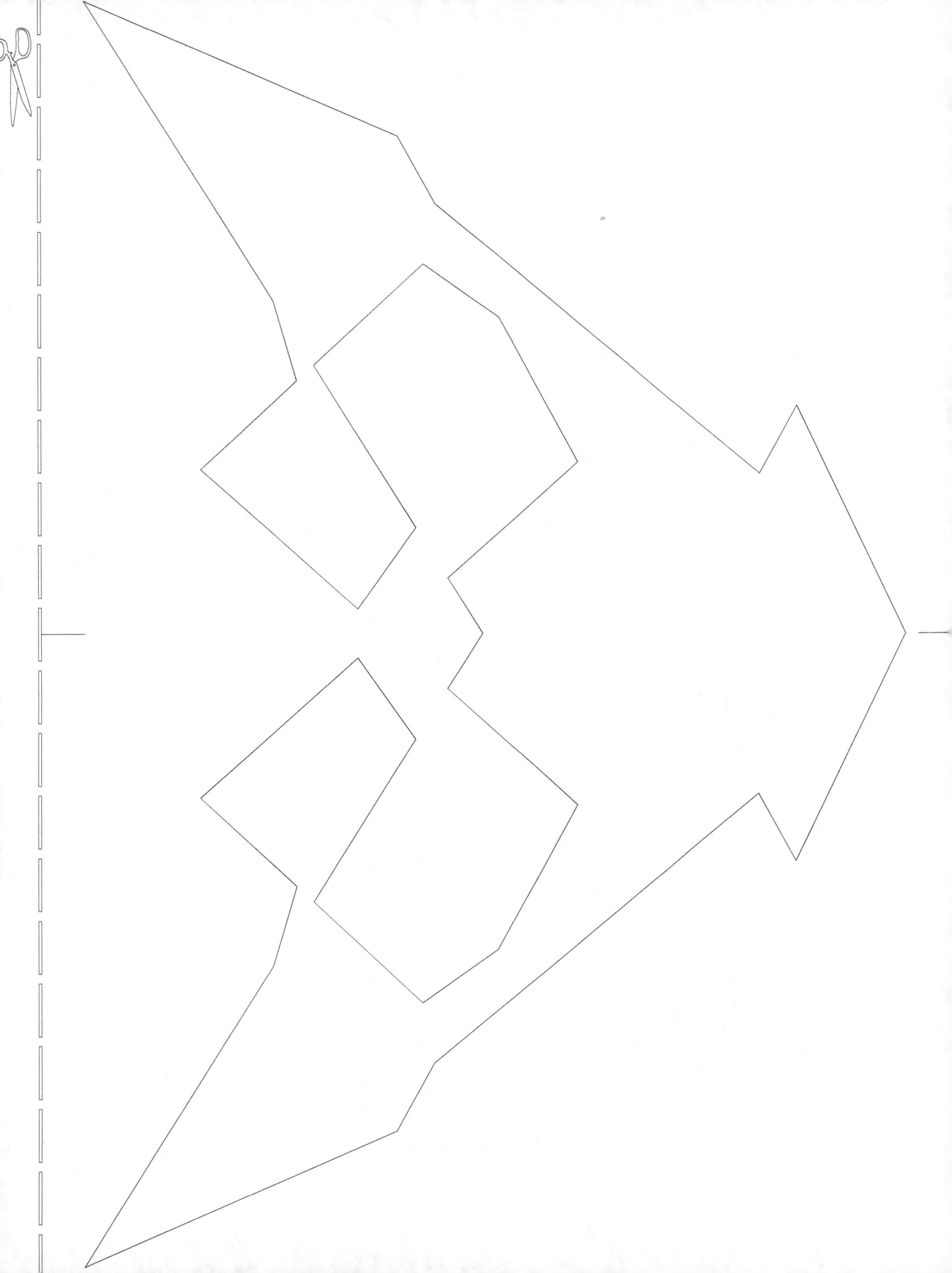

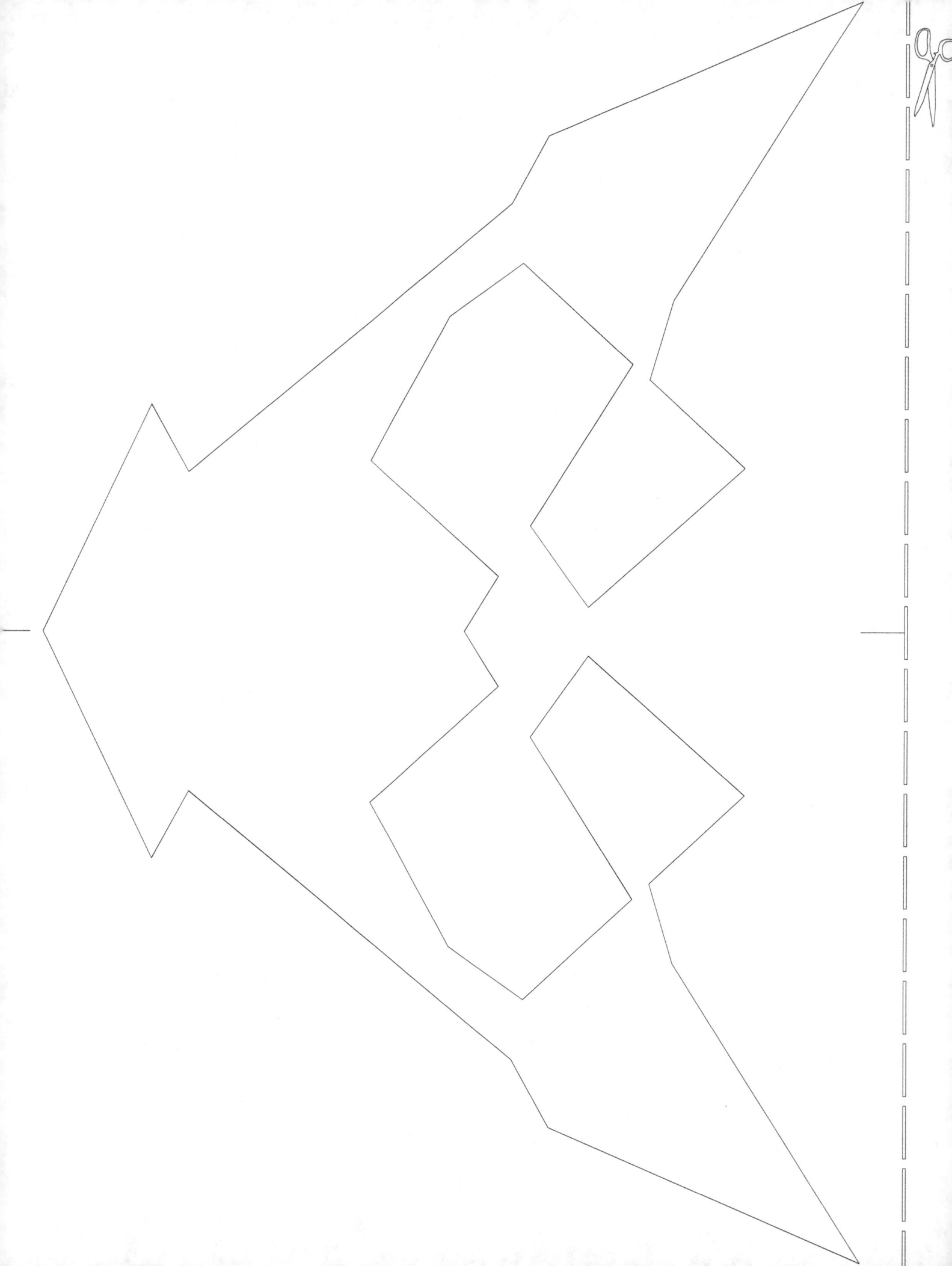

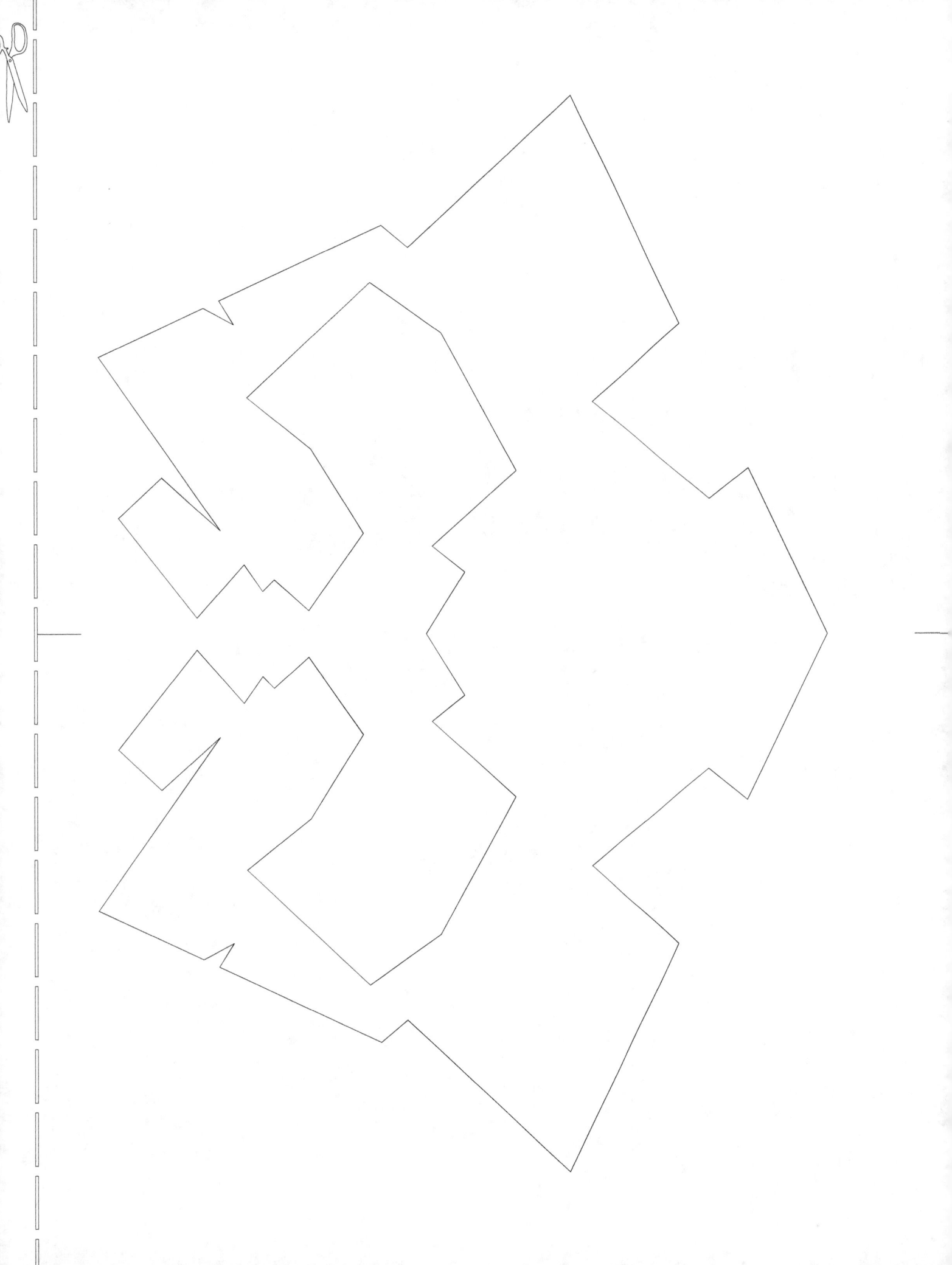

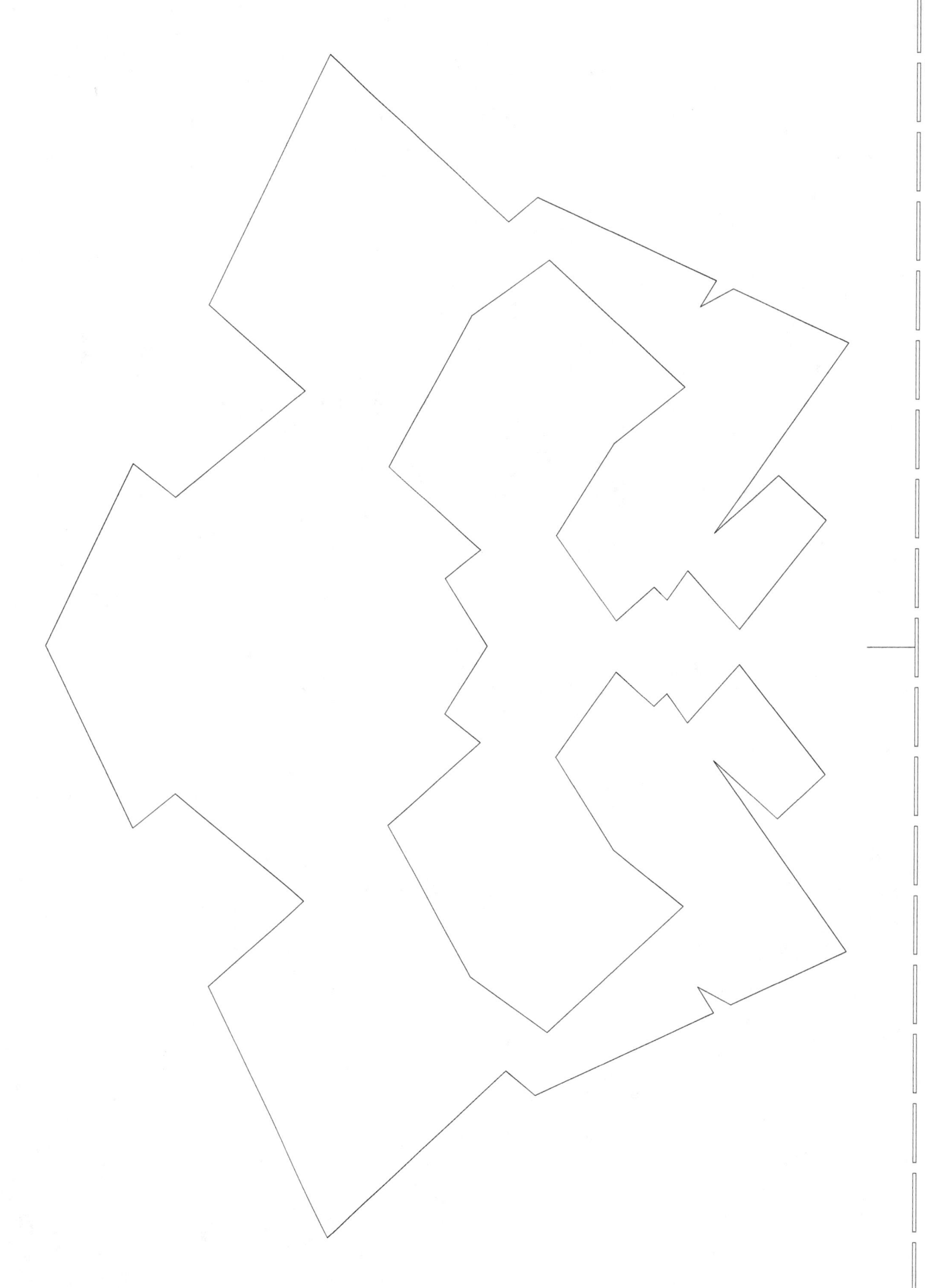

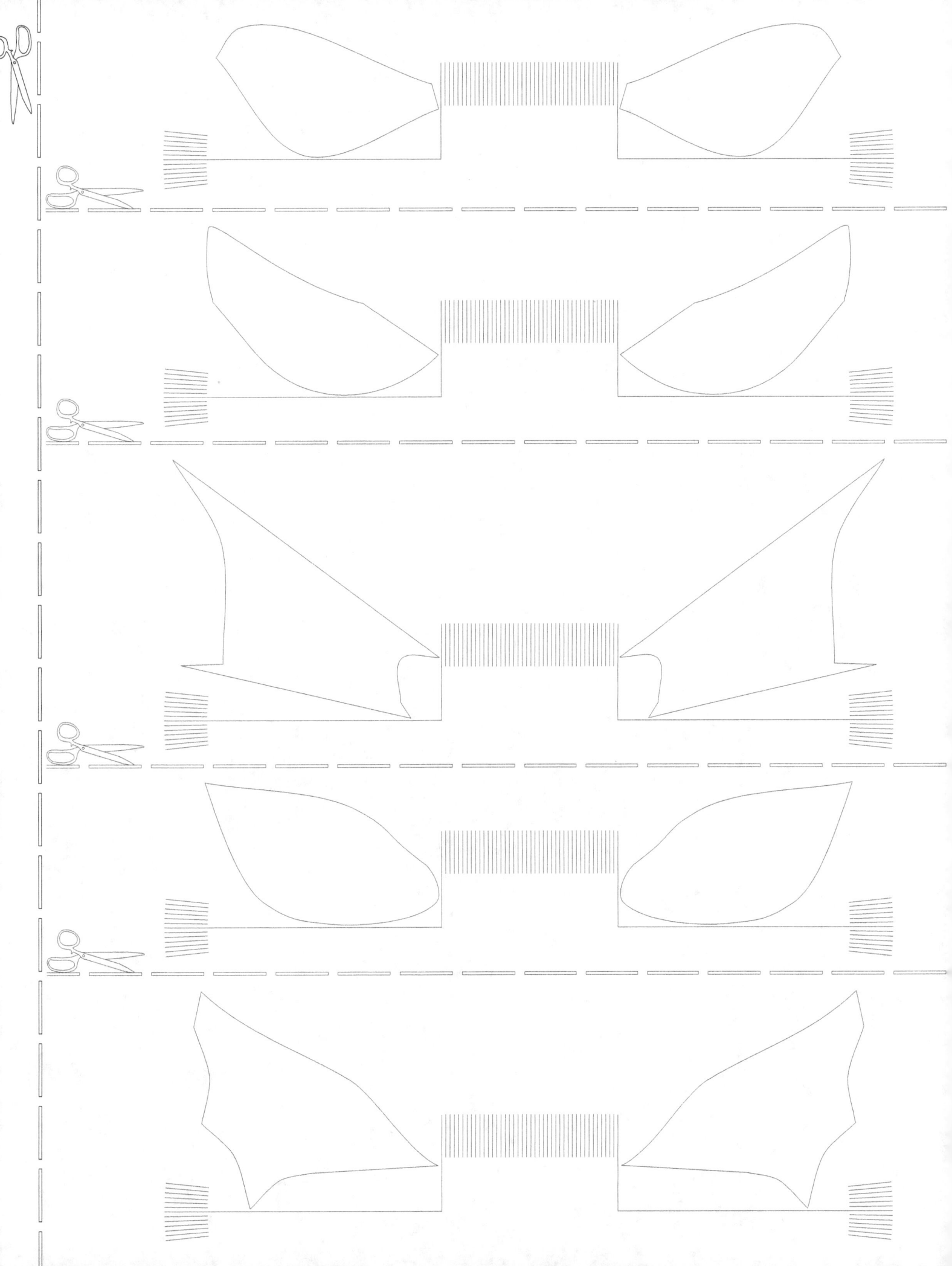

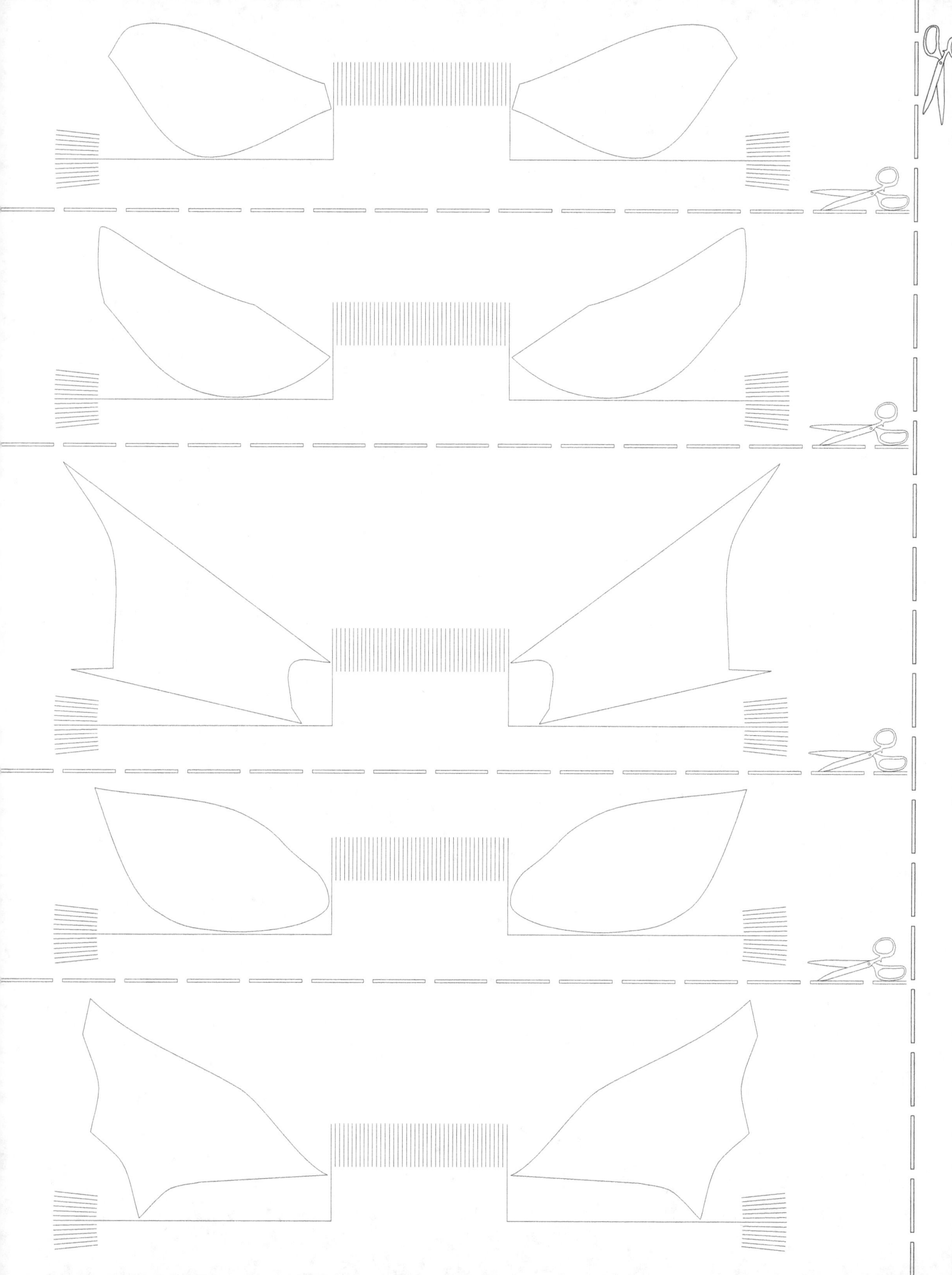

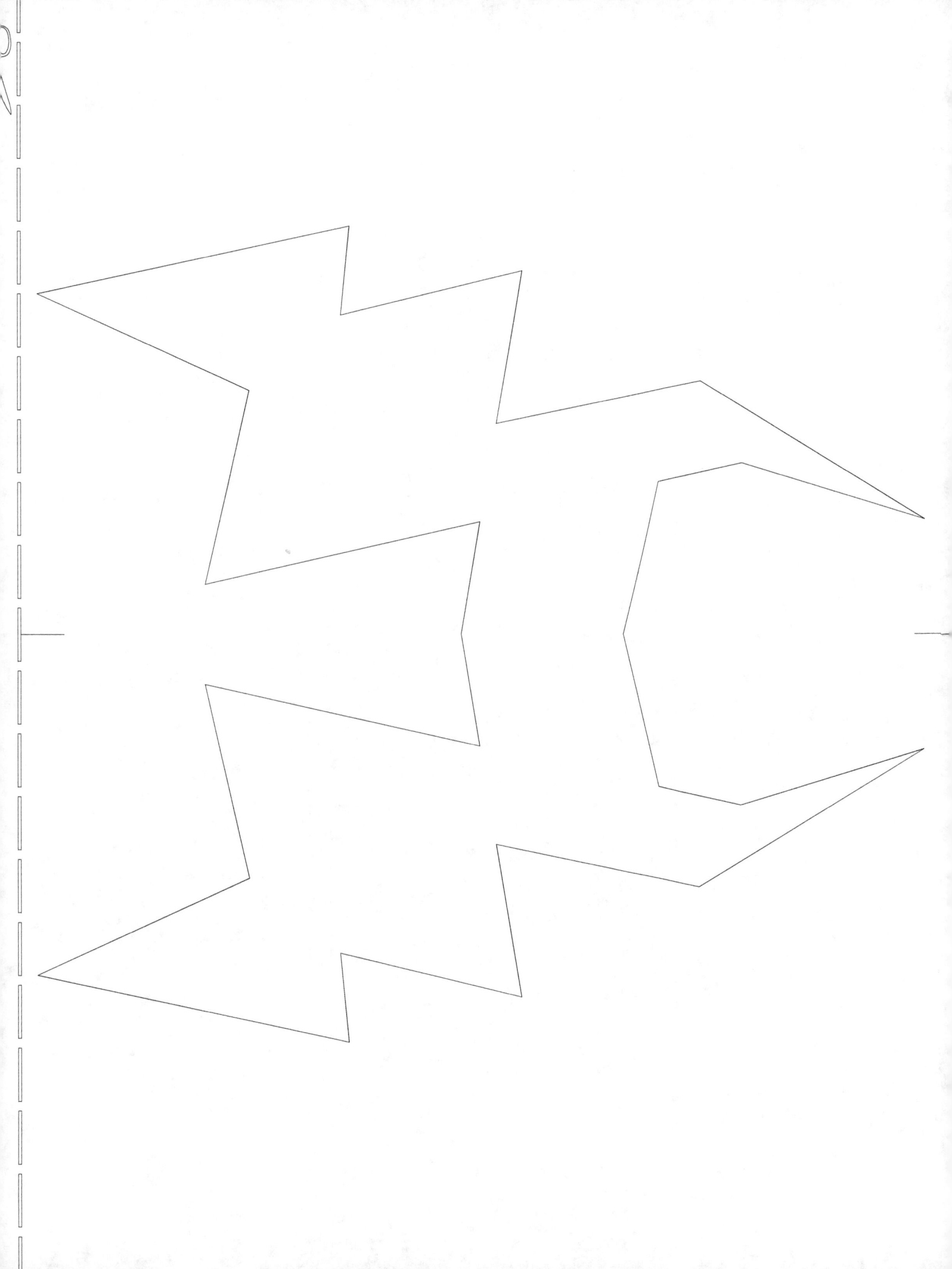

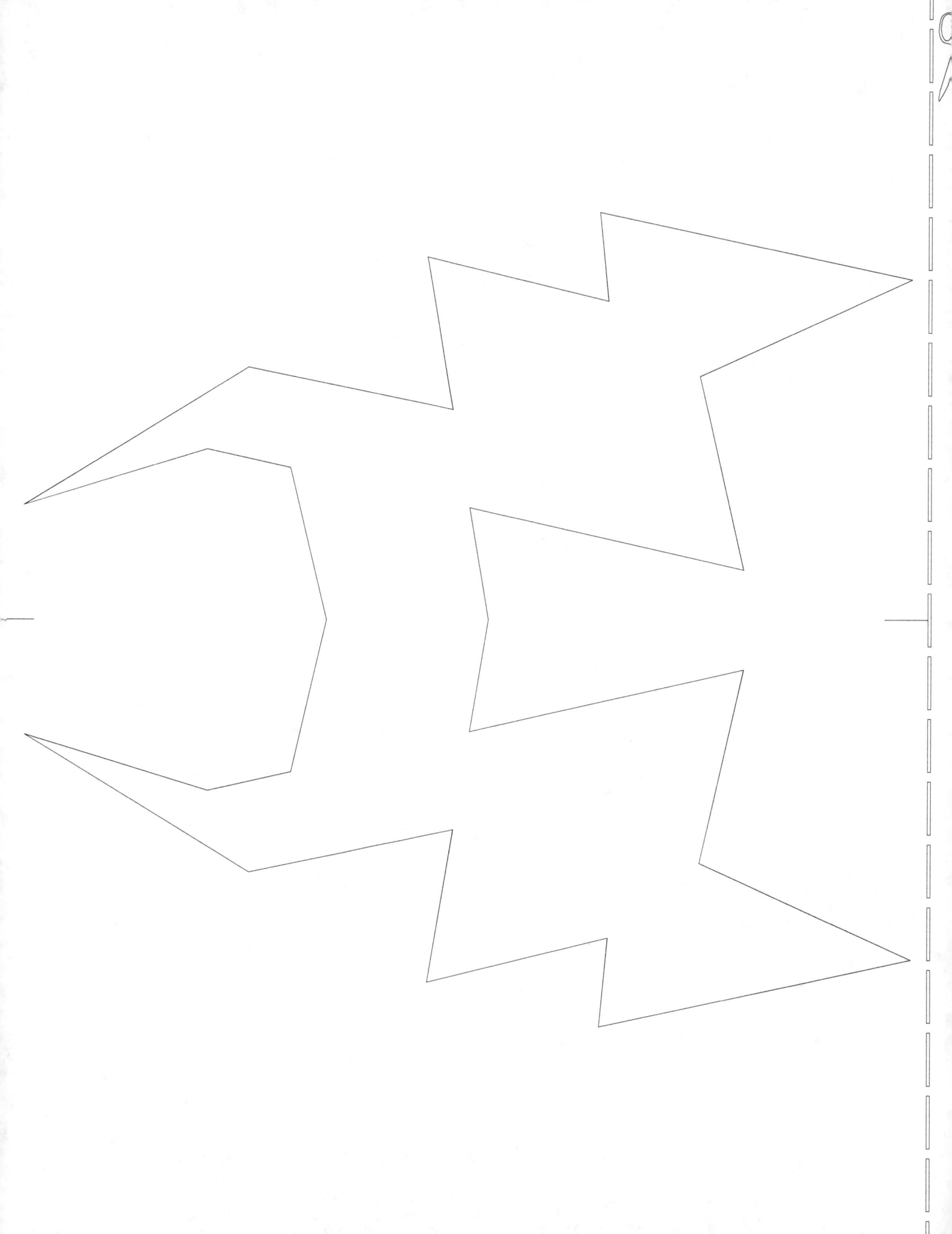

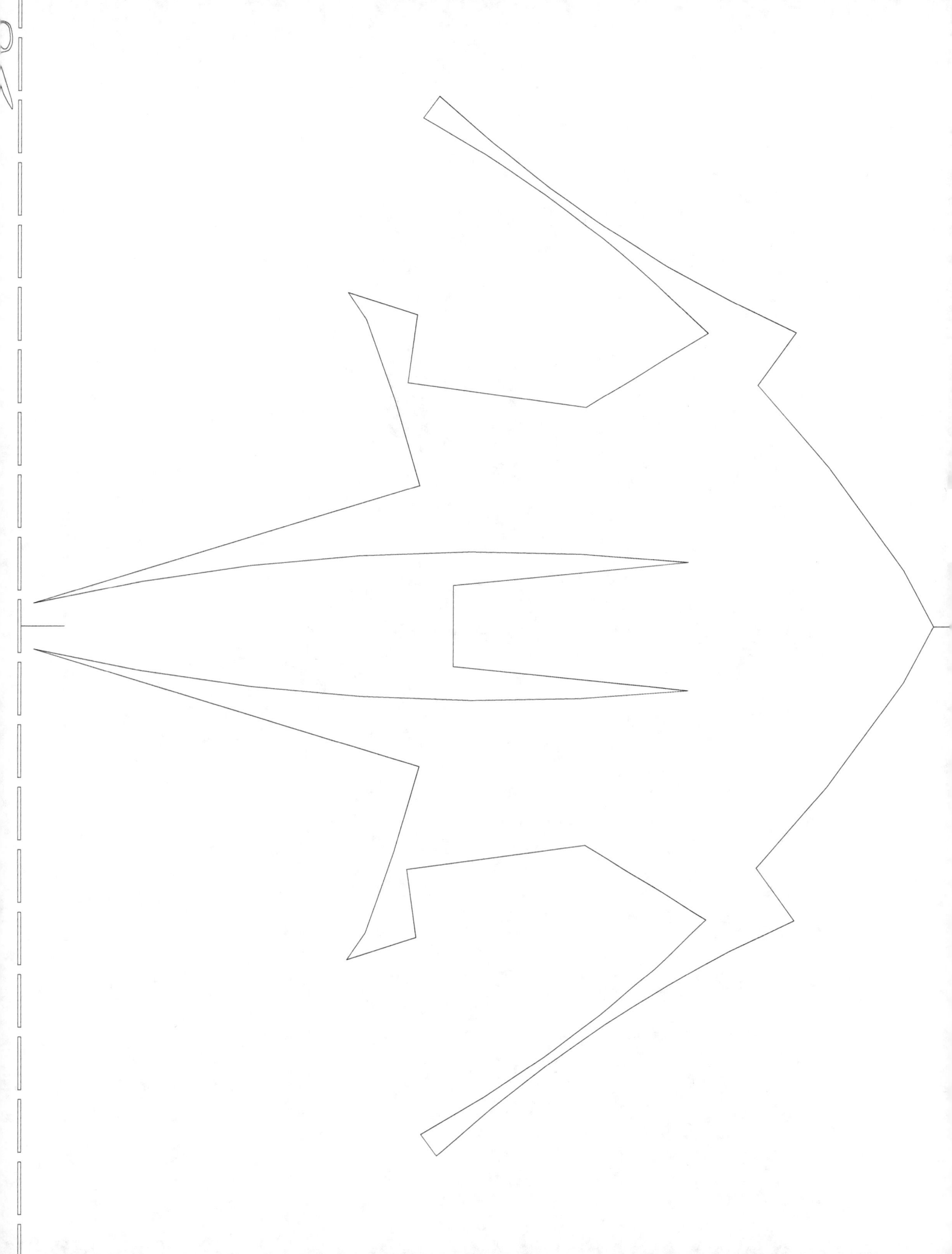

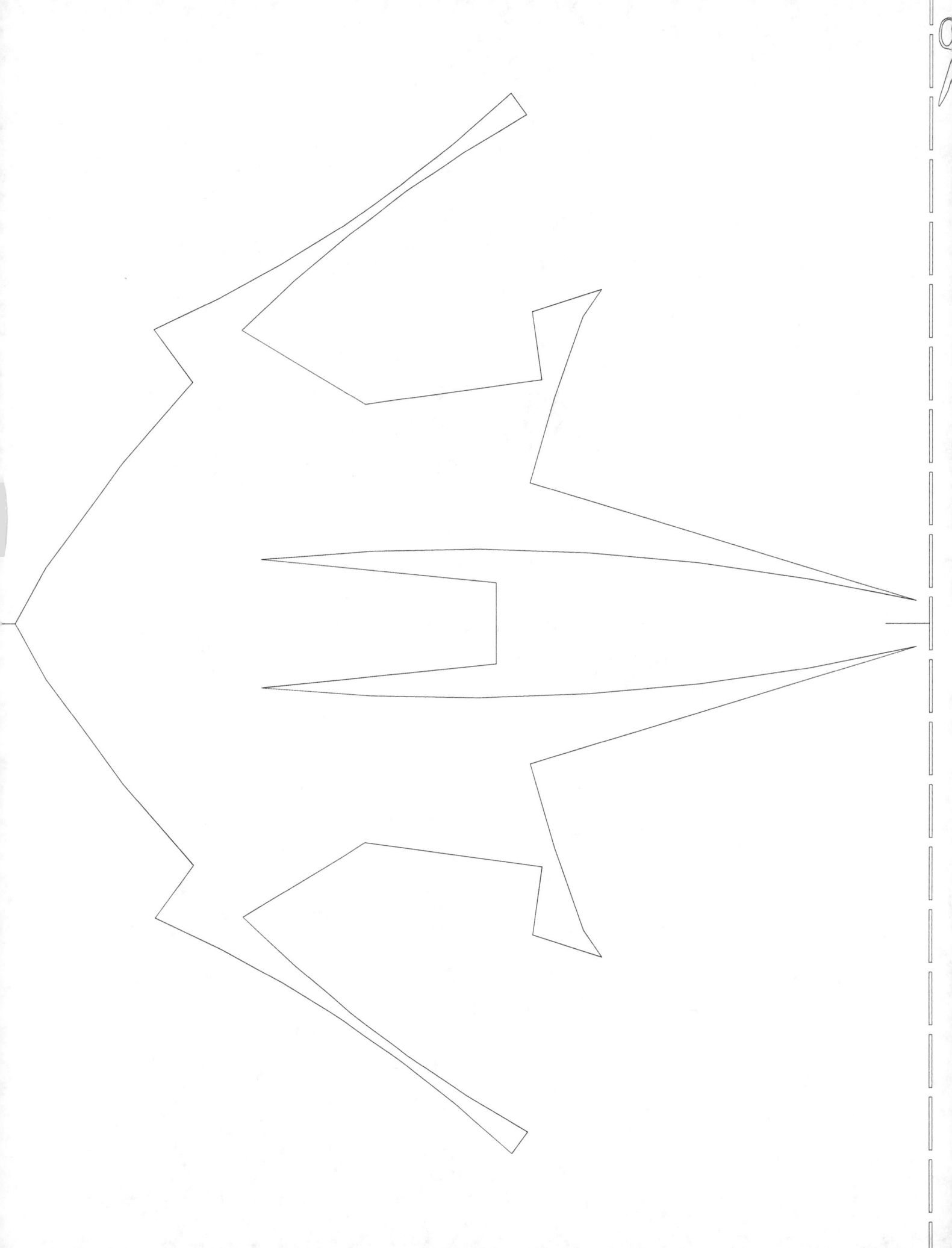

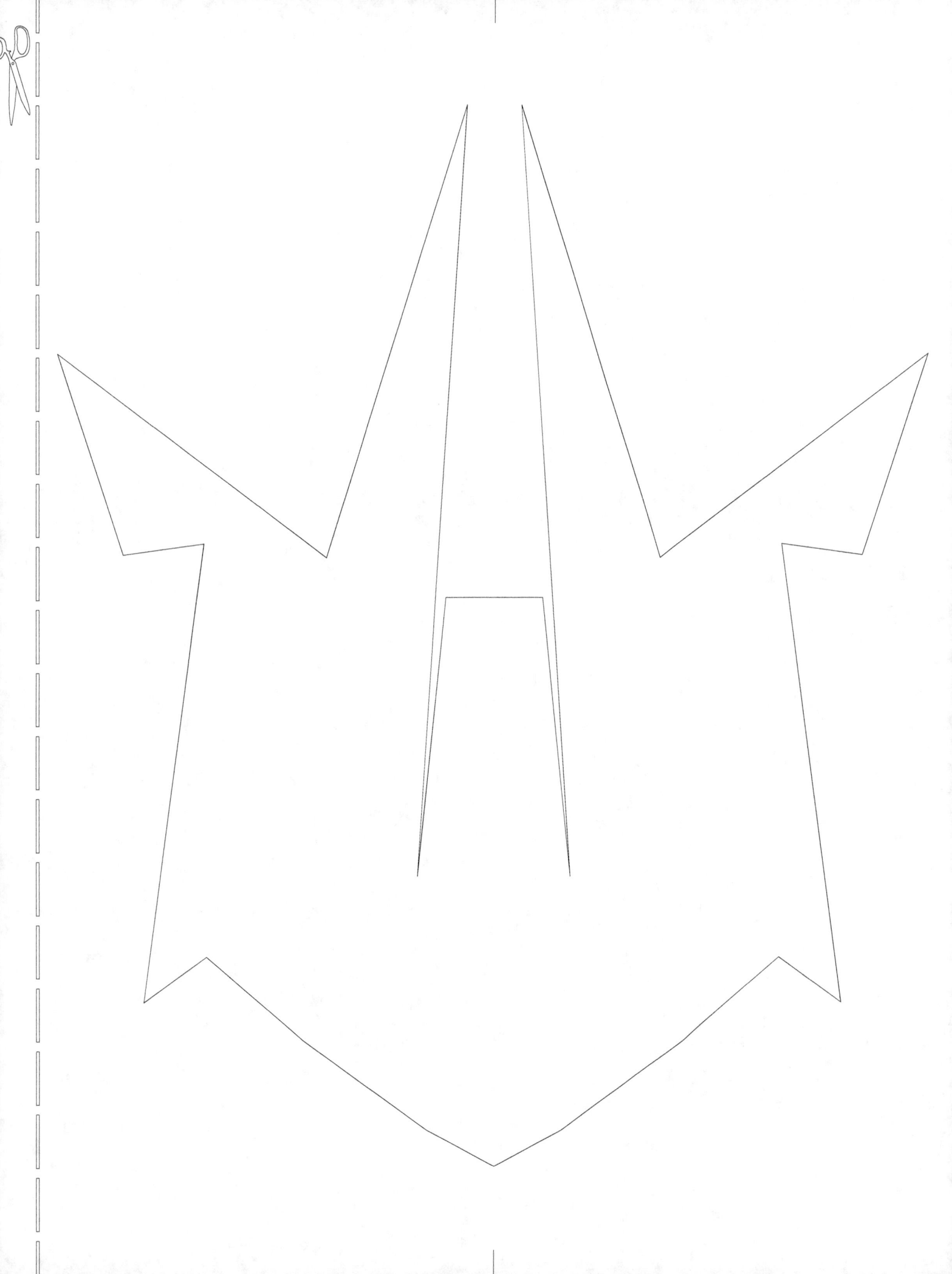

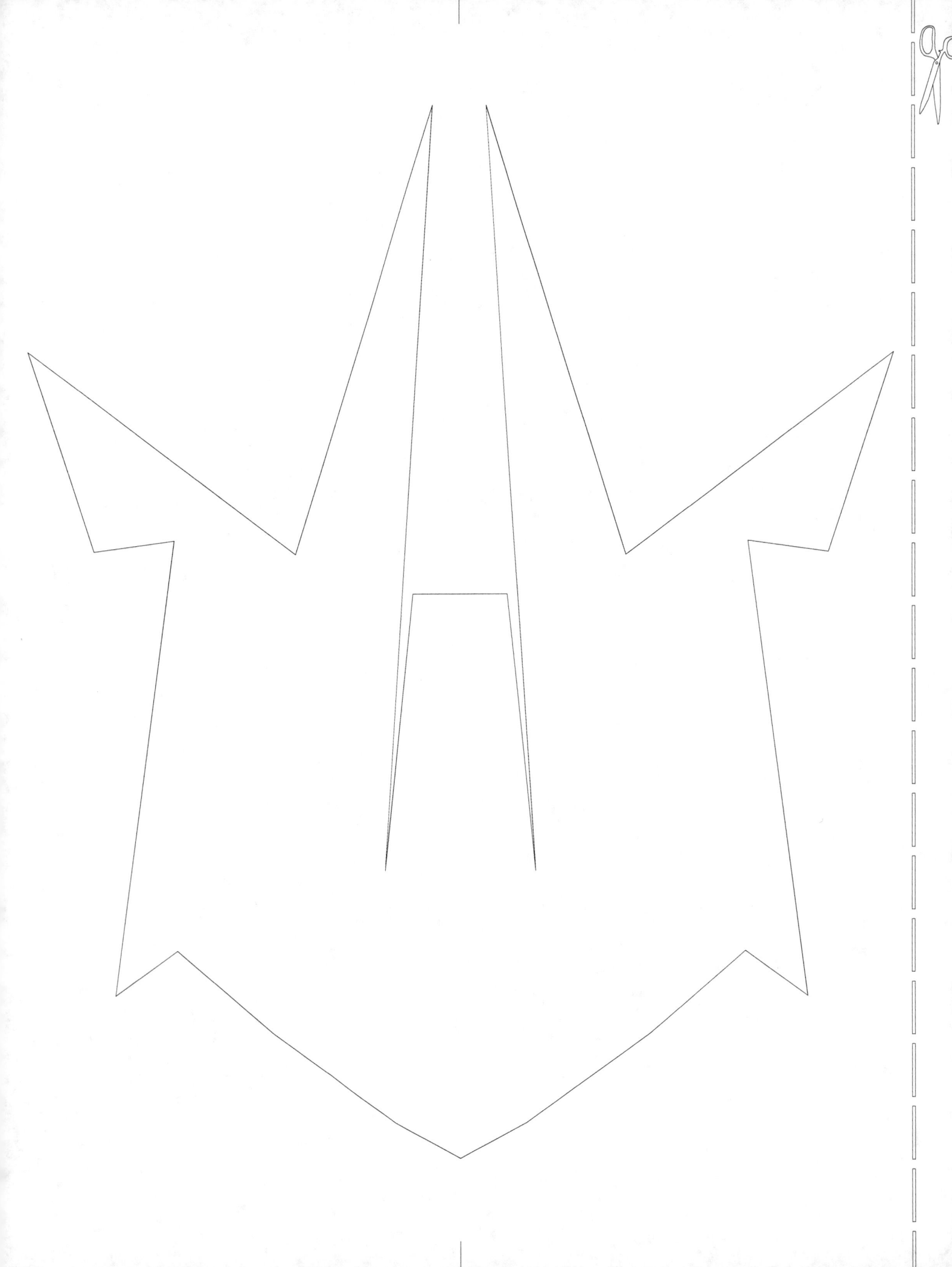

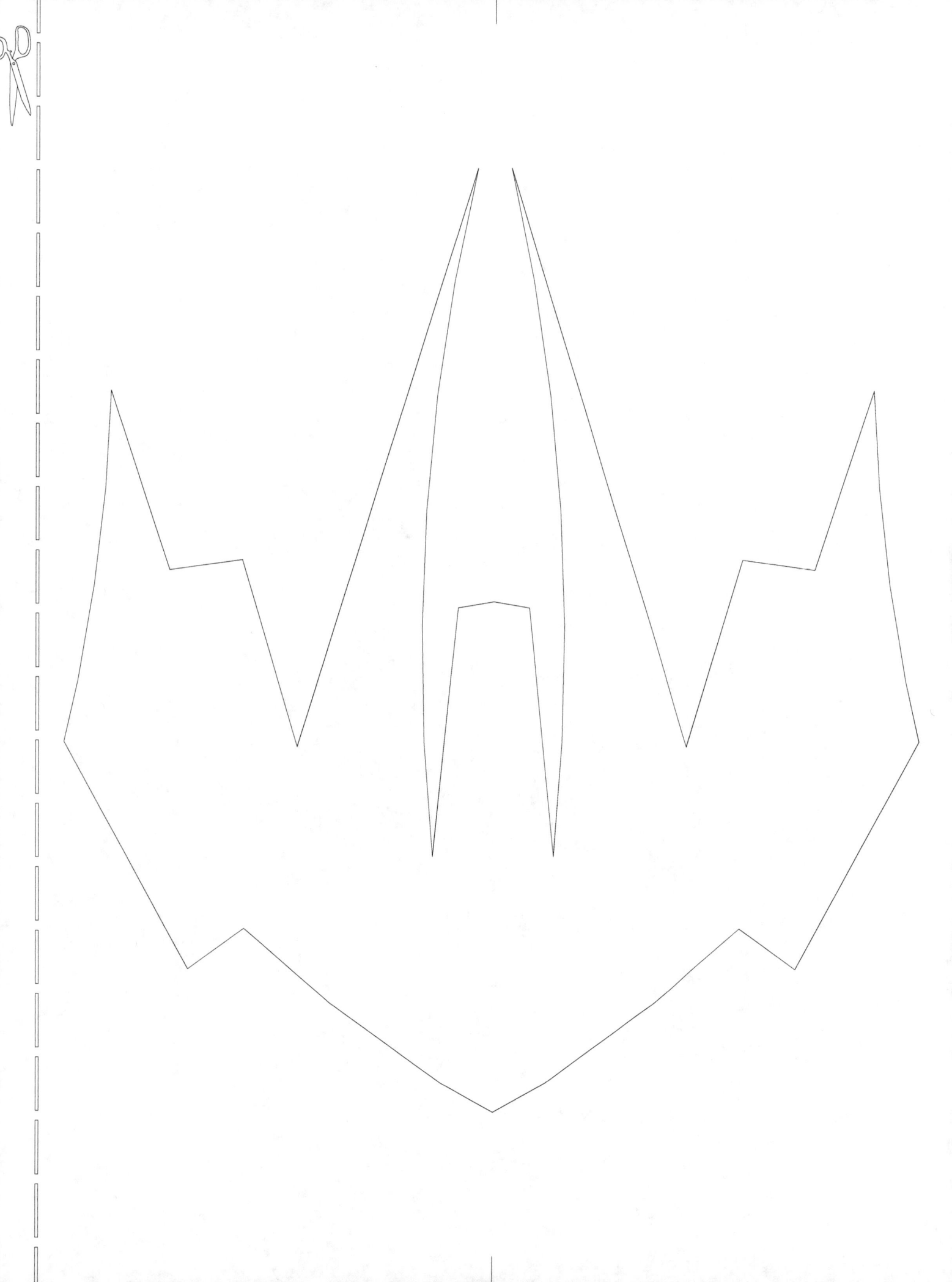

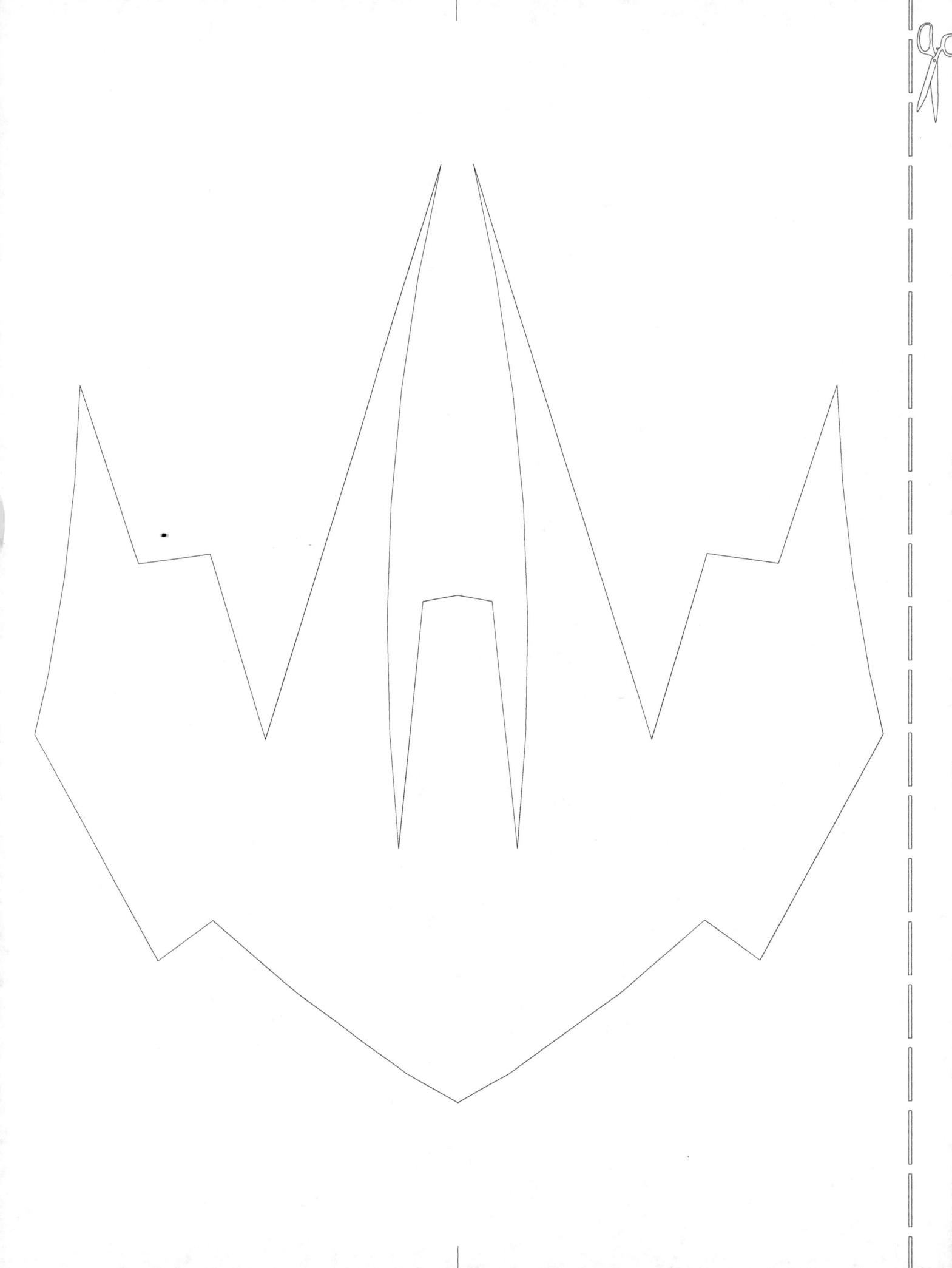

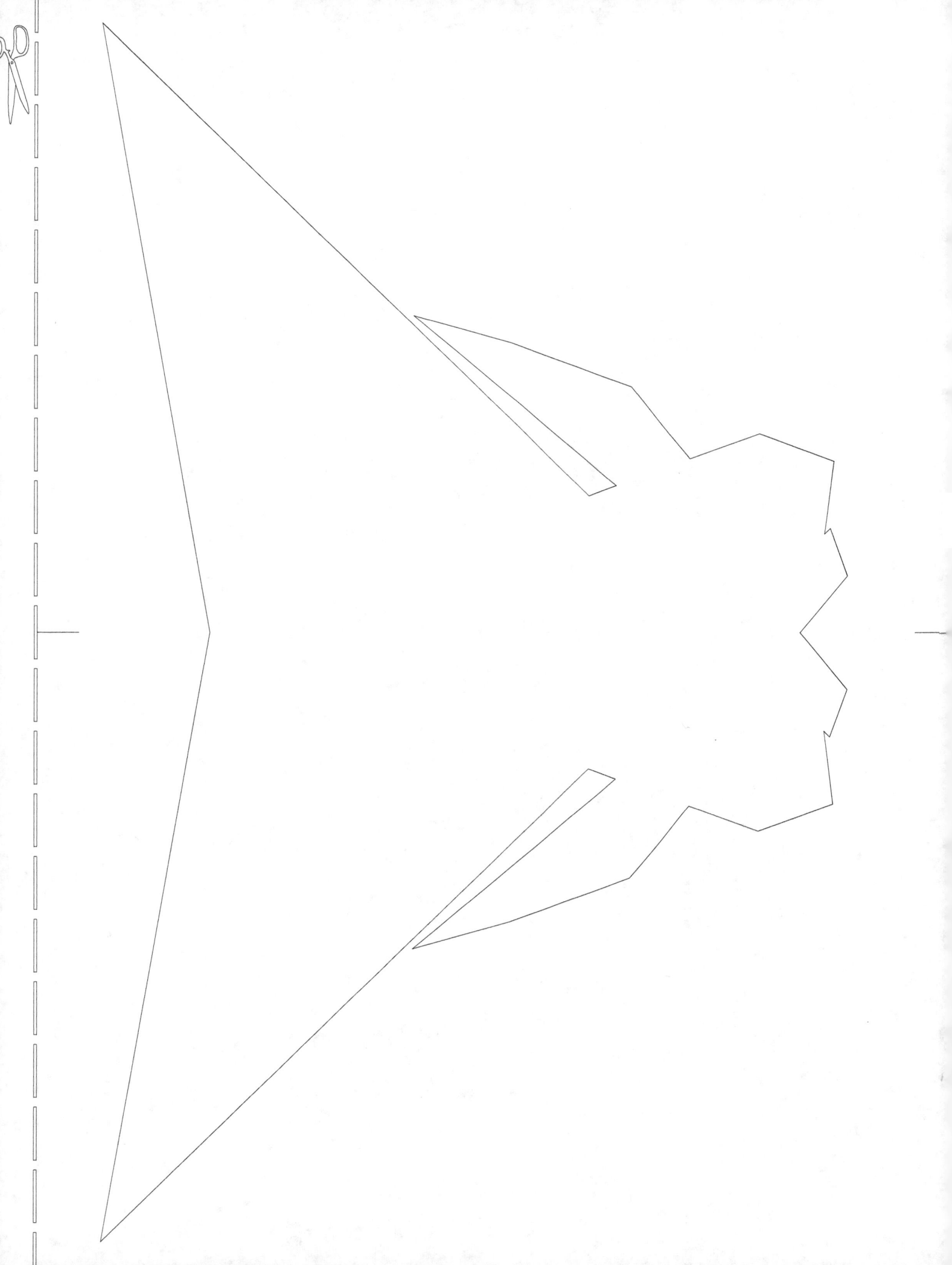

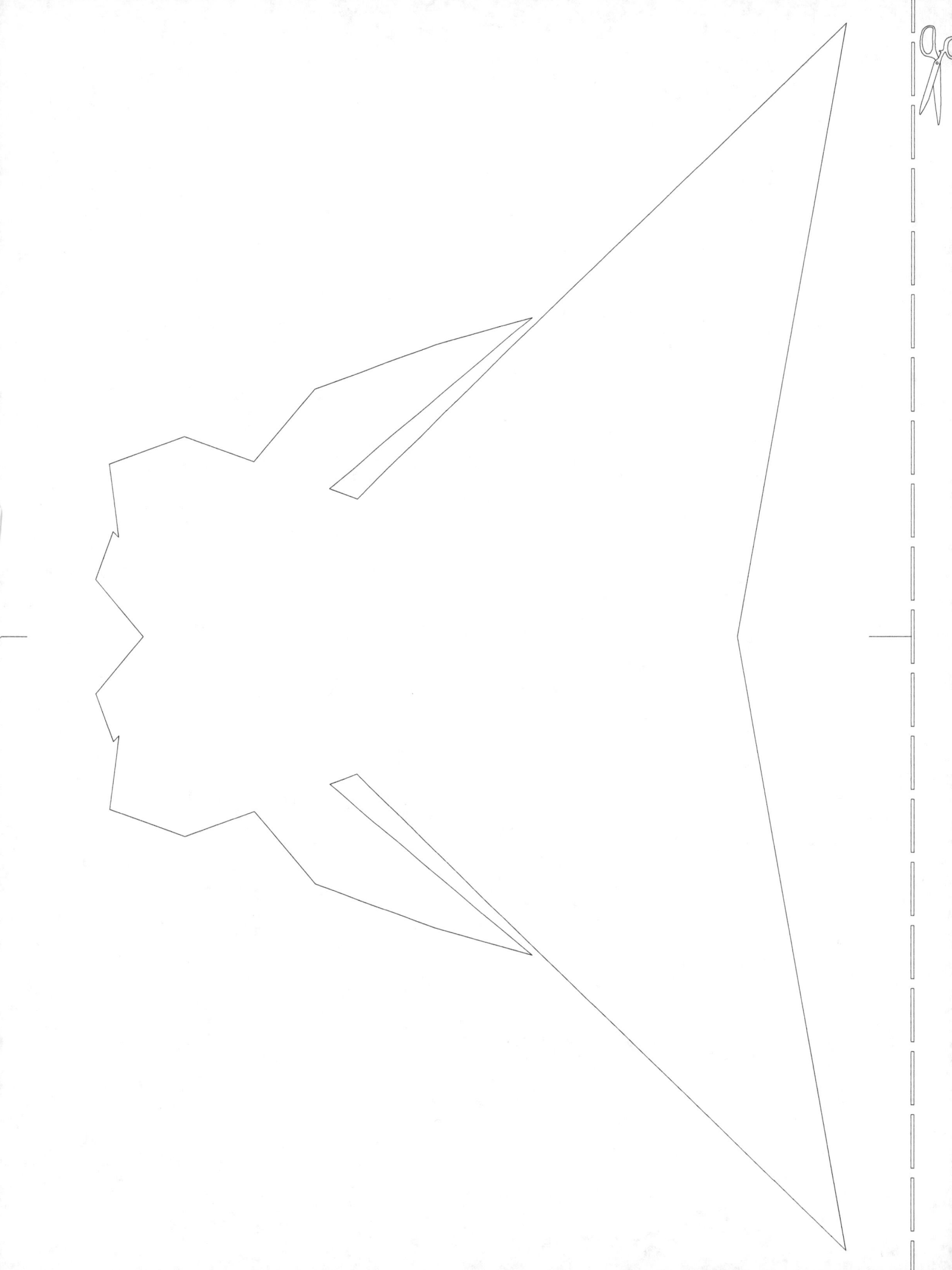

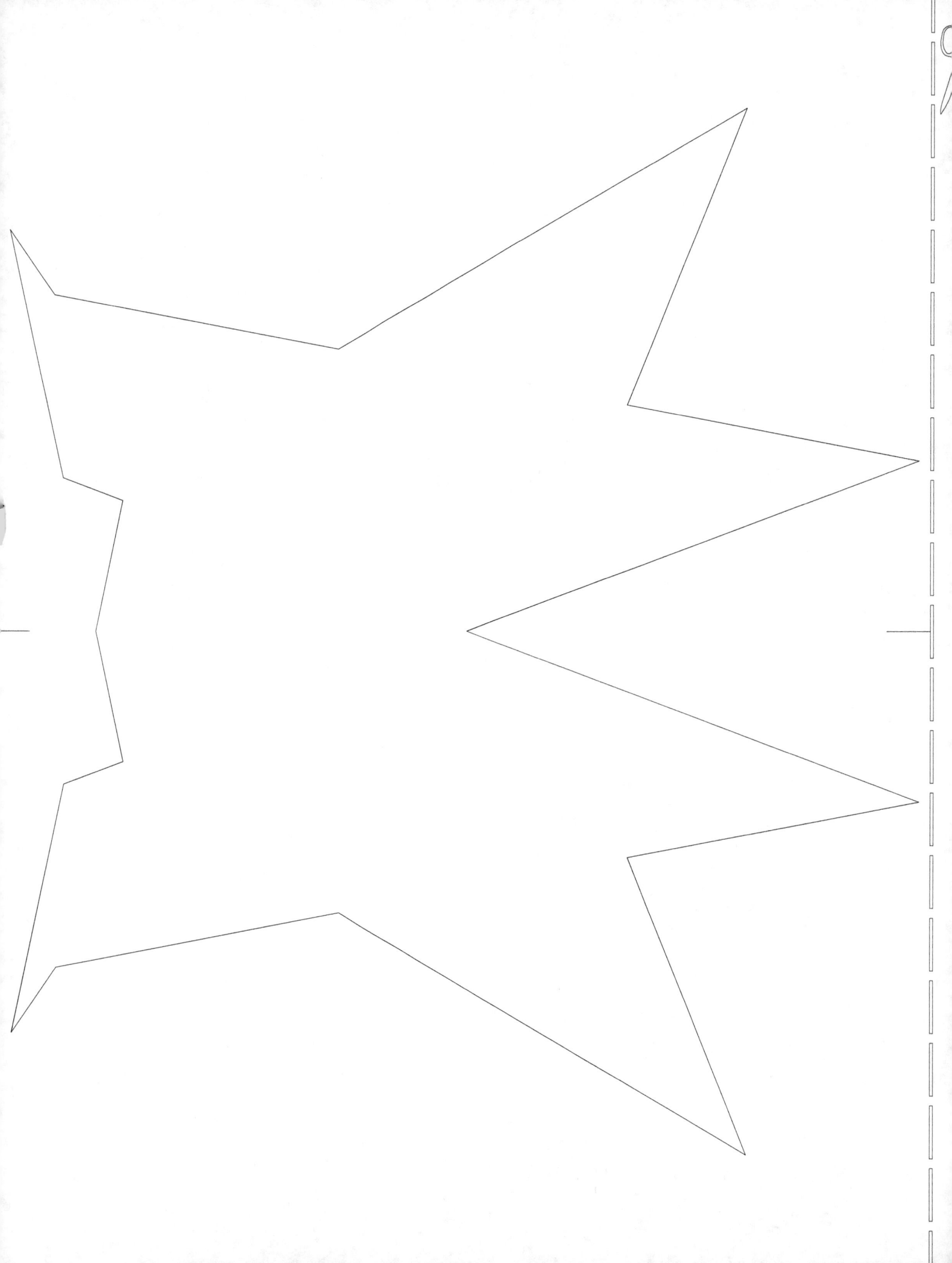

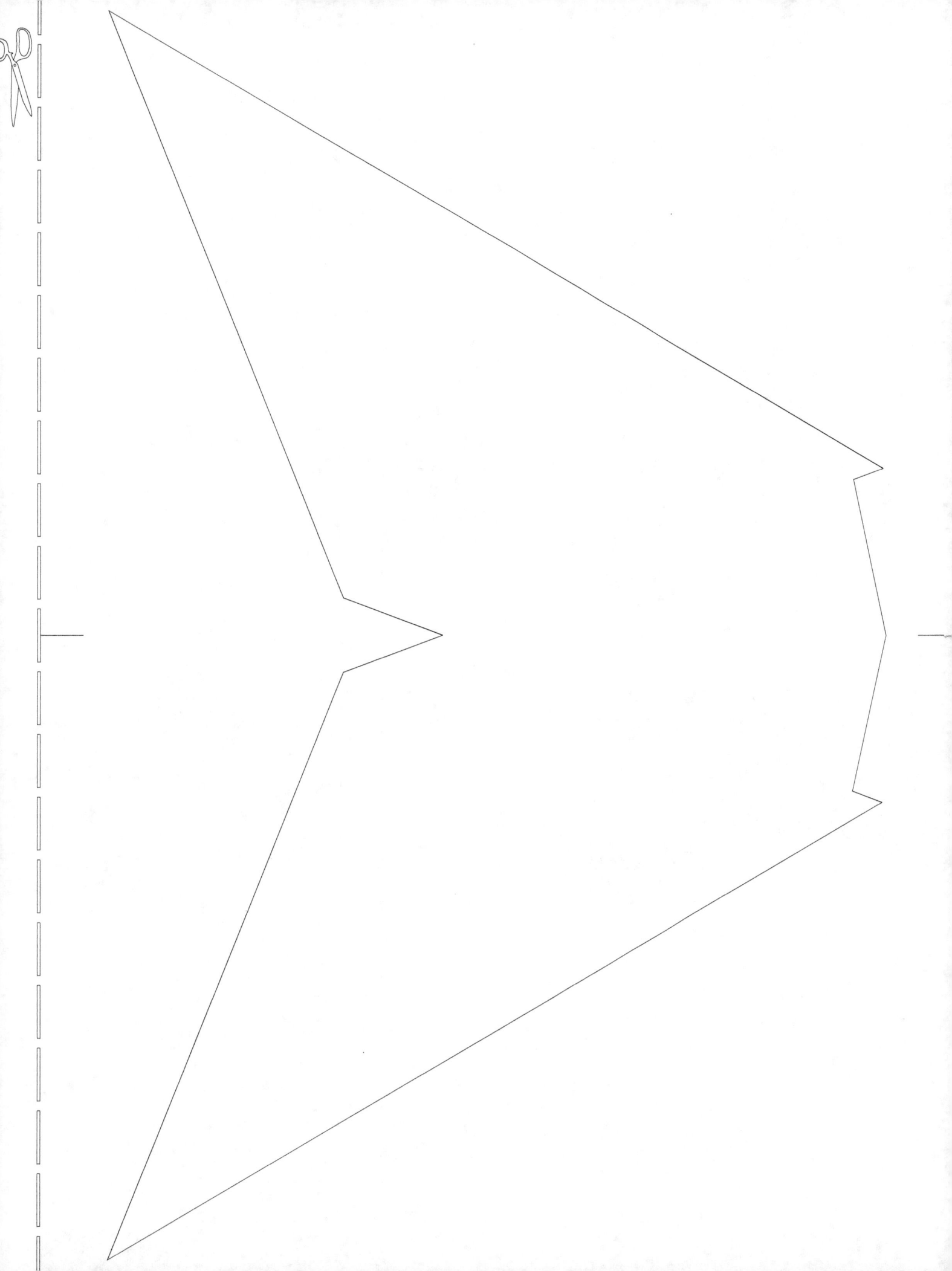

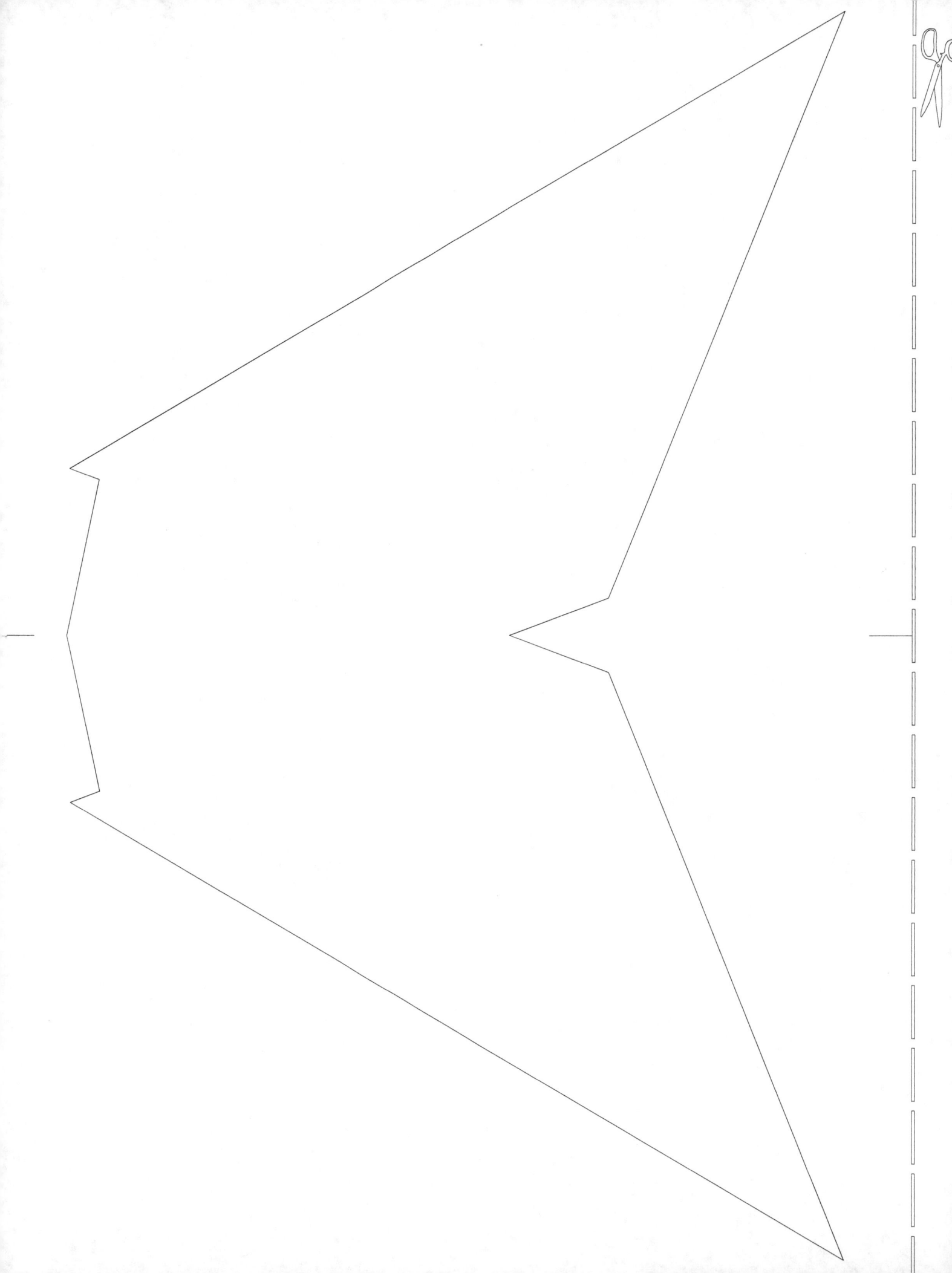

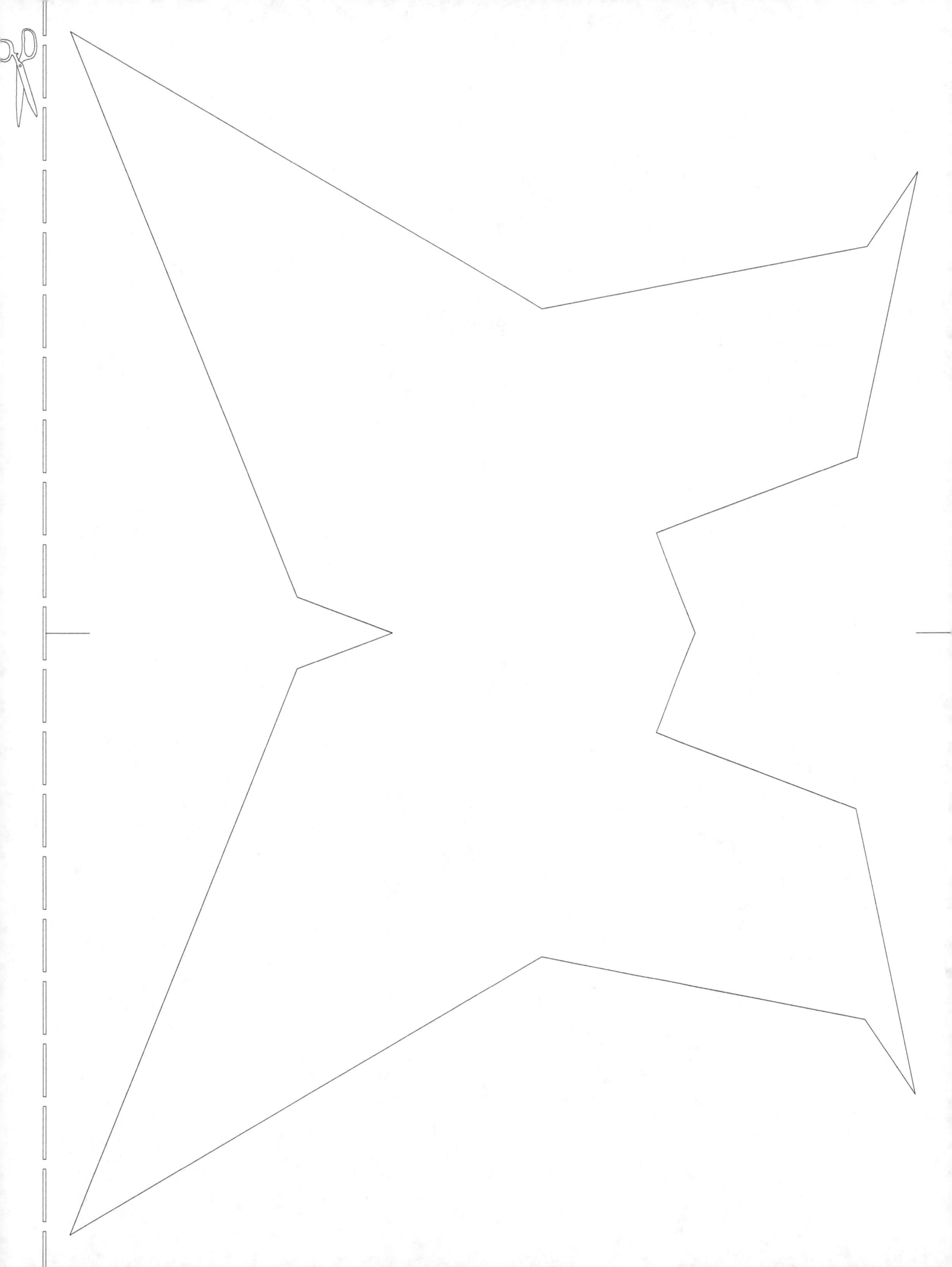

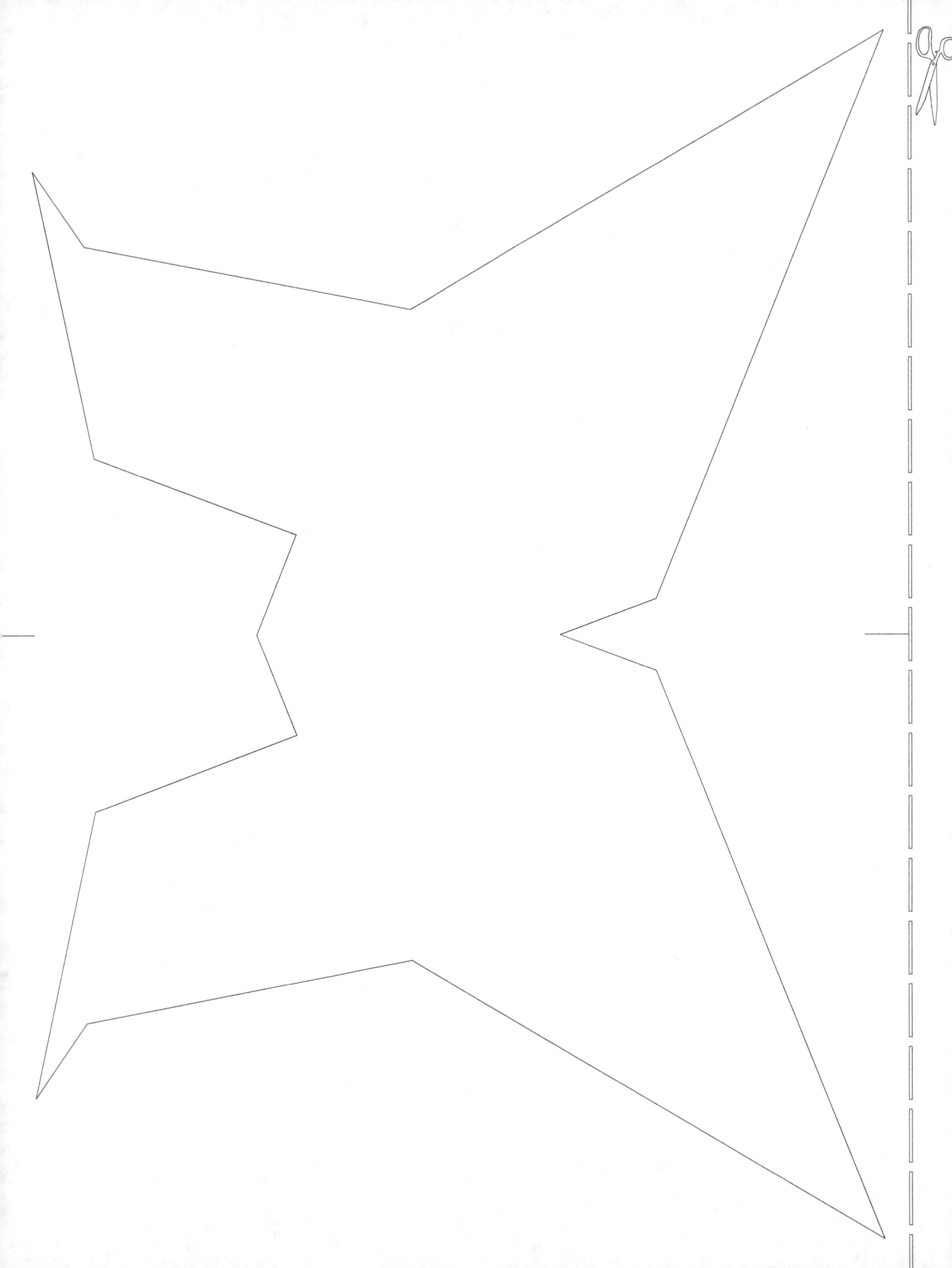

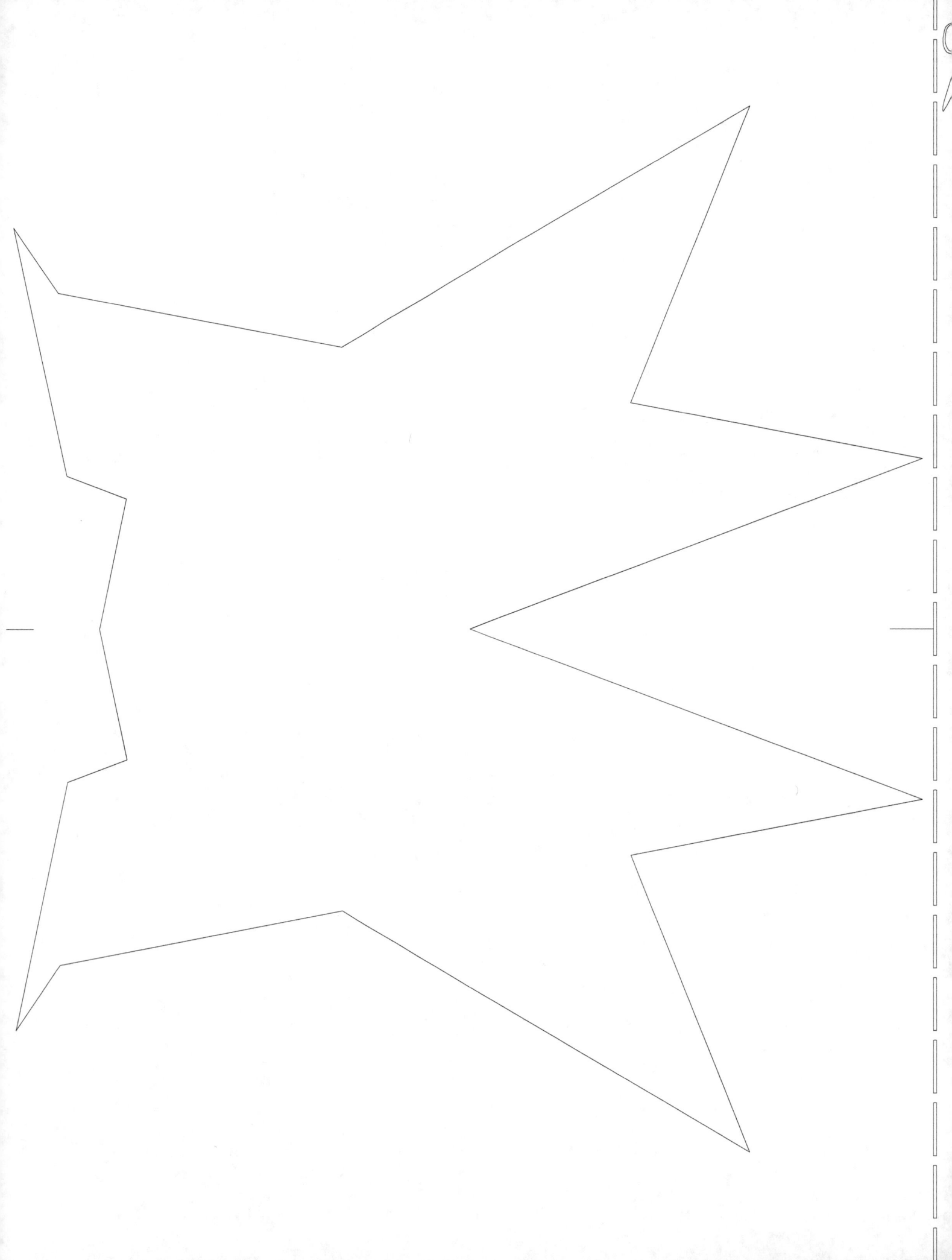

www.ingramcontent.com/pod-product-compliance
Lightning Source LLC
Chambersburg PA
CBHW080853170526

45158CB00009B/2722